The Life and Times of
HENRY VIII

The Life and Times of
HENRY VIII

Robert Lacey

Introduction by Antonia Fraser

CROSS RIVER PRESS
A division of Abbeville Press, Inc.
NEW YORK

First published in the United States,
1992, by Cross River Press, a division
of Abbeville Press, Inc., 488 Madison
Avenue, New York, NY 10022.

First published in the United Kingdom, 1972,
by George Weidenfeld and Nicolson Ltd.

© George Weidenfeld and Nicolson Limited
and Book Club Associates 1972, 1992

Series designed by Paul Watkins

ISBN 1-55859-451-5

Introduction

THE LARGER-THAN-LIFE SIZE figure of Henry VIII straddles across the stage of English history, dominating us as in his famous portraits by Holbein. Indeed, if we think of his amazing vigour – the agile athlete of his youth, whose fair skin glowed through his tennis shirt, the skilful knight who loved to take part anonymously in tournaments – we seem to have the very pattern of majesty, as the role should be played, in an age when the attributes of the monarch were all-important. For Henry in his splendour could be equally effective: under his auspices took place the great Field of the Cloth of Gold, 'the eighth wonder of the world' as it was termed at the time, and this was also the period of more durable creations such as Nonsuch Palace and Hampton Court. Nor were Henry's excellent brain and his genuine appreciation of music mere minor qualities puffed up by the praise of courtiers. Henry in the first years of his reign could fairly claim to be a prodigy of intelligence, energy, and with his bright auburn-haired good looks, even of beauty: 'the handsomest potentate in Europe' as a contemporary called him.

It is just because this noble dawn gave way to a blood-stained sunset, with old friends such as Bishop Fisher and More put to death and the people's tragedy of the Pilgrimage of Grace, that Henry remains one of the most controversial of our monarchs, as well as having a strong claim to be the best known. Not all this fame accrues from his marital record, although that has understandably seized the popular imagination: the proud and virtuous Spanish Princess Catherine of Aragon, humiliatingly cast aside for her failure to produce a male heir; sloe-eyed Anne Boleyn (whom the populace more crudely termed 'the goggle-eyed whore'); sweet Jane Seymour doomed to an early grave, where Henry ordered himself to be laid beside her after death, a tribute to the one love that never turned sour; the over-homely Anne of Cleves; and finally those two contrasts of his last years, wanton, plump little Catherine Howard, and the prudent Catherine Parr, already twice-widowed, whose wisdom enabled her to survive even this most difficult of husbands. Quite apart from such colourful marital junketings, the importance of Henry's reign in our history is immeasurable, since within its confines took place the Reformation, which exchanged an international Church subordinate to Rome for a State Church under the headship of the King. And yet even here, we cannot avoid the contemplation of the King's own headstrong personality, since this State Church was rooted in Catherine of Aragon's failure and Anne Boleyn's triumph.

Sir Thomas More compared the King when young to the king of beasts, adding presciently: 'If a lion knew his strength, it were hard for any man to hold him.' To go further, in all the political shifts of the reign, the changeover in the system of administration, the work of Wolsey and Cromwell, the pursuit of a cripplingly expensive foreign policy too often involving war, one can never leave out of one's calculations the character of this 'lion' who stood at the centre of it all. In Henry's reign all roads led to and from the throne, and it is because Robert Lacey never loses sight of the magnetic figure of the King, threading his way clearly through all the tangled events which surrounded him, that he is able to produce such a lively and stimulating narrative of Holbein's baleful but ever fascinating hero.

Antonia Fraser

Acknowledgments

Photographs and illustrations were supplied or are reproduced by kind permission of the following. The pictures on pages 10–11, *14–15/1, 14–15/2, 34–5, 46–7,* 49, 53, 69, 72, 83, 89, 102–3, 105, 139, *141, 144/2,* 164/1, 174, 178/1, 178/2, 178/3, 207, 211, are reproduced by gracious permission of H.M. the Queen; on page 23 by courtesy of the Dean and Chapter of Westminster; on page 50 by kind permission of the Earl of Yarborough; on pages 73, 112 and 119 (below) by permission of Lord Astor; on page 114 by permission of M. Ward Thomas, Esq; on page *144* (below) by courtesy of the Archbishop of Canterbury (Copyright reserved by the Courtauld Institute of Art and the Church Commissioners); on page 170 (below) by permission of Mrs J. B. More-Molyneux: on page 197 by courtesy of the National Trust; and on page 213 by permission of His Grace, the Duke of Norfolk. Aerofilms Limited: 159/1; Annan: 202–3; Archives Photographiques: 58–9; Ashmolean Museum, Oxford: 164/2; Barber Surgeons' Company: 82/2; Batsford: 165; Bibliothèque de Méjanes, Aix-en-Provence: 13/2; Bodleian Library, Oxford: 42, *80/1, 80/2,* 82/1, 88; British Museum: 26/1, 26/2, 28–9, 36, 48, 57, 63, 96, 100–1, 110, 118, 122, 170–1, 172–3, 183/2, 194, 198, 216–7; Courtauld Institute: 197; Department of the Environment: 32, 114 (Crown Copyright), *132,* 158, 183/1; Fitzwilliam Museum, Cambridge: *3;* Raymond Fortt: 214; Frick Collection, New York: *129;* Gabinetto Fotografico: 179; Herbert Gernsheim: 168–9; Giraudon: 51; Ian Graham: 167; Michael Holford: 90–1; A. F. Kersting: 75; Kunsthistorisches Museum, Vienna: *65, 77/2;* Kunstmuseum, Basle: 18–19, 175; Kunstsammlung, Basle: 78–9; Lambeth Palace: *144/3;* David Lipson: 114; Louvre, Paris: *68,* 124–5, *144/1;* Magdalen College, Oxford: 16; Mansell Collection: 66, 51; Mauritshuis, The Hague: 90; Paul Mellon Collection: 124–5; Musée Condé, Chantilly: 51; National Galleries of Scotland: 204; National Gallery: 177, 180–1; National Monuments Record: 27/1, 165; National Portrait Gallery: 2, 13/1, 41, 67, *77/1,* 131, 142, 153, 180, 187, 188–9, 206–7; La Pensée Universitaire: 13/2; Portsmouth City Museums: 184–5; Prado, Madrid: 90–1; Public Record Office: 98, 154; Radio Times Hulton Picture Library: 38–9, 84, 148, 215; Royal College of Arms: 30, 60–1; Scala: 76; Tom Scott: 10–11; Staatliche Museen, Berlin: 134; *The Times:* 119/2; University Press, Oxford: 16; Vatican Library: 74–5; Victoria and Albert Museum: 27/2, 119/1, 120–1, 123, 127, 159/2, 212; Warburg Institute: 168–9; Yale University Library: 95.

The author owes acknowledgment to the following for quotations and conclusions: J. Scarisbrick, *Henry VIII,* Eyre & Spottiswoode (Publishers) Ltd: A. F. Pollard, *Henry VIII,* Longman Group Limited: Sir Arthur McNalty, *Henry VIII, a difficult patient,* Johnson Publications Limited.

Picture research by Jasmine Spencer.

1
The Renaissance Prince
1491-1514

As no one expected Henry to become King of England, his early youth was not closely reported by the chroniclers who traditionally chart the progress of heirs to the throne. They either amuse or annoy us with the sycophantic inaccuracy of their prophesies, but in this case they might at least have provided us with some clues towards an understanding of how Henry VIII came to be the remarkable man that he was. He was only the third child of Henry VII, himself an unexpected King, who had, against all odds, risen from being a minor exiled earl to topple the crown from the head of Richard III at Bosworth Field on 22 August 1485. Hard-headed and calculating, Henry VII knew how fortunate he was to be sitting on the throne of England, and how lucky he would be if he stayed there. Legality had had nothing to do with it. His great-grandfather had been a fugitive Welsh brewer wanted for murder: his grandfather had had the temerity to seduce the French widow of Henry V. Through his mother he had only an illegitimate connection with John of Gaunt, Richard II's uncle. So, to make sure that his children, at least, were blessed with royal blood somewhat thicker than his own, one of Henry VII's first acts was to seal a marriage for himself with Elizabeth of York, the daughter of Edward IV.

From this marriage came Arthur, the first-born and eldest son, a handsome, sensitive boy who promised all the great things that his Christian name deliberately claimed for him. Malory's *Morte D'Arthur* was published in the year Henry VII seized the throne, and was a best-seller throughout the reign. Then came Margaret, rapidly betrothed and married to King James IV of Scotland – the marriage from which the Stuart kings, and indeed the Union of England and Scotland, were later to spring. After Margaret, on 28 June 1491, was born in the Greenwich Palace the son named after his father. And then came another daughter, Mary, and two more sons, insurance policies against the vagaries of Renaissance medical science.

In the event, it was Henry who won through the lottery of royal mortality that was to trouble him so greatly in later life. For, whereas Henry VII triumphed handsomely in guaranteeing that he would be succeeded by a strong male heir, that heir was not so fortunate, and the story of his reign became, in many ways, the story of his increasingly desperate efforts to emulate his father's powers of procreation.

PREVIOUS PAGES Henry VII and his family with St George and the Dragon. Henry and Elizabeth of York are shown kneeling with their seven children, three of whom did not survive infancy. On the tents behind them are the Tudor rose and the Beaufort portcullis. Henry VII's mother, Margaret, was the last of the Beauforts.

12

On 14 November 1501, at the age of ten, the young Henry attended the wedding celebrations of his elder brother Arthur. He headed the procession which led Arthur's bride to St Paul's Cathedral, and, after the ceremony, he led her out to meet the cheering crowds of London. There followed ten days of rejoicing. Henry VII might be careful with his money, but when lavish expense was called for, he could be prodigal. The ten-year-old Prince demonstrated a lively enthusiasm for the mummings and games that made up the celebrations; everyone remarked particularly on the relish with which he danced. This was a sign of things to come, and the identity of his brother's bride was even more portentous, for she was called Catherine of Aragon – the daughter of Ferdinand and Isabella of Spain.

Soon this proud Spanish Princess came to loom large in the life of young Henry Tudor, for Arthur was dead within four months of the marriage, and Henry was suddenly heir to the throne of England. He succeeded to his brother's wife as well.

ABOVE LEFT Henry VII, painted in 1505, by an unknown artist.
ABOVE RIGHT A drawing of Henry VIII as a baby.

13

The meeting between Henry VIII and the Emperor Maximilian I, during their war against France in 1513. Behind the sovereigns and their entourage can be seen the allied cavalry clashing with the French.

The Battle of Spurs, which took place in August 1513. In this scene, the English and Imperial troops are putting the French to flight.

That, at least was the plan. A treaty was signed with Spain on 23 June 1503 providing that Henry, then a week short of his twelfth birthday, should marry when he reached his fifteenth year, on 28 June 1505. Catherine would then be nineteen, older than her husband but not too old, and her parents should, in the interim, send over to England one hundred thousand crowns' worth of plate and jewels – a substantial wedding portion.

The least complication seemed at the time to be the theological obstacles to a man marrying his brother's widow. Catherine claimed, almost indignantly, that her marriage to Arthur had never been consummated. The boy had been very ill, and Catherine's duenna, a ferocious lady called Doña Elvira, backed up her young charge. If the ladies were correct, then there was

no real barrier to the marriage with Henry. All that was needed was a 'Dispensation from the Impediment of Public Honesty' – little more than an extended calling of the banns.

But old Henry VII wanted to be absolutely sure his heir's connection with the power and influence of Spain was unshakable, and, before they paid over the huge dowry demanded, the Spaniards for their part wanted to be quite sure that the English had no excuse for wriggling out of the match at the last minute. So Catherine's assertion was ignored. It was assumed that her marriage *had* been consummated, and the whole problem was referred to the Pope. After months of waiting – a matter of crude delay, rather than of deliberation – the Holy Father spoke: he sent to London a dispensation stating that despite the affinity between them, Henry and Catherine might wed.

The one remaining problem was that the new marriage portion due from Spain had not been paid, so, though Henry referred to Catherine as 'my most dear and well-beloved consort, the princess my wife', his father allowed him to see little of her, and refused to allow the couple's union to be solemnised, let alone consummated. To help prise the desired money out of Spain's coffers he even got his son to make a formal protest to Richard Fox, Bishop of Winchester, disowning the marriage contract and promising never to marry the Spaniard. Doubtless the intention was to wave this in the face of the Spanish ambassador on the next occasion that he proved particularly obstinate over the payment of the dowry, but, as matters turned out, it was not produced until a much later date and for an altogether different purpose. For on 22 April 1509 old Henry VII died and the new King, who cared far more to have a strapping wife in his bed than a few thousand extra crowns in the Exchequer, married Catherine of Aragon almost as quickly as he could.

The Spanish ambassador, Fuensalida, most agreeably surprised by this haste after long months of delays and haggling, noted shrewdly the somewhat strange fashion in which the seventeen-year-old Henry VIII had been prepared for his inheritance. His father had given him no taste of power or responsibility – it was almost as though young Henry was not a prince but a princess, to be kept shut up out of harm's way.

OPPOSITE Detail from an early sixteenth-century Flemish tapestry, now in Magdalen College, Oxford, showing the betrothal of Arthur Prince of Wales and Catherine of Aragon. Richard Mayhew, President of the College from 1480 to 1506, was one of the envoys sent to meet the Spanish Princess when she arrived in England in 1501 to marry Prince Arthur.

Either because of Arthur's death, or possibly because he felt his second son was able enough to do without the experience, Henry VII had made no attempt to send his heir down to Wales. In London he was only allowed out in the company of carefully selected tutors and guards – and then only through a special private door into the royal park. The only access to his rooms was through the chamber of Henry VII himself, and when the King produced his son in public he allowed him to speak to no one. His voice was only heard when he answered, docilely, his father's questions.

Of course, there was every reason why Henry VII should make it difficult for the Spanish ambassador to get close to the young heir, and Fuensalida needed every excuse to explain, when he wrote home to Catherine's father, Ferdinand, why he was failing to engineer the definite union between the Princess and young Henry. Yet there can be little doubt that Henry VII was a strict father, and the exuberance with which Henry VIII, like the cork from a champagne bottle, exploded into his new inheritance in the spring of 1509 suggests that his youthful development had been more than a little repressed. At all events, he soon made up for lost time.

England was delighted with her handsome young King – and understandably so. He was a prodigy which the chilly offshore island could proudly show off to the rest of Europe. Lord Mountjoy wrote delightedly to Erasmus of Rotterdam: 'I have no fear but when you heard that our Prince, now Henry the Eighth, whom we may well call our Octavius, had succeeded to his father's throne, all your melancholy left you at once.' (Erasmus, for all his philosophy, was rather a hypochondriac, and suffered from agonising bladder stones.) 'What may you not promise yourself from a Prince with whose extraordinary and almost Divine character you are acquainted?' Erasmus had met the new King when Henry had been only ten, had thrown together some little poems for the Prince, and had written to him since.

When you know what a hero he now shows himself [went on the rapturous Mountjoy] how wisely he behaves, what a lover he is of justice and goodness, what affection he bears to the learned [Erasmus was always on the look-out for wealthy patrons] I will

venture to swear that you will need no wings to make you fly to behold this new and auspicious star. If you could see how all the world here is rejoicing in the possession of so great a Prince, how his life is all their desire, you could not contain your tears for joy. The heavens laugh, the earth exults, all things are full of milk, of honey, of nectar! Avarice is expelled the country. Liberality scatters wealth with bounteous hand. Our King does not desire gold or gems or precious metals, but virtue, glory, immortality.

Those final words were pointed and precise, chosen with a good deal more care, we may well feel today, than the euphuistic praise that preceded them. For Henry VIII was not simply a bright new monarch – rare has been the king or queen who has not enjoyed upon their accession some sort of honeymoon with their people – he succeeded a man who had been bitterly, if somewhat unjustly, despised as a miser. And as a significant pointer to the less sunny side of the new King's nature, his first reaction to the one and a quarter million pounds left him by his father was not gratitude to the men who had helped gather it, but eagerness to kow-tow to the popular dislike of the financial efficiency of the previous reign.

A royal proclamation was issued inviting anyone in the kingdom to come and charge the late King's servants with extortion – though Henry had chosen his victims already: Sir Richard Empson and Edmund Dudley. They had been particularly zealous servants of Henry VII – and had made many enemies in the process. The trouble was, of course, that they had been acting on the dead King's specific instructions and had no difficulty in proving this. So a totally fictitious charge of treason was concocted and the men were savagely and unjustly tried, sentenced and executed.

In the later years of Henry VIII's reign such cold-blooded judicial murder became a commonplace, and it has been suggested that this blood-thirstiness was a reflection of Henry's increasing age, power and problems, that circumstances rather than character provide the explanation for the autocratic ruthlessness that flourished so spectacularly as he grew older. But the victimisation of Empson and Dudley, and the surgical skill with which their destruction was legalised, argues otherwise. Henry cut them down with the ease and lack of qualm that a Borgia would have been proud of. In 1513, about to

Page from the *Stultitiae Laus*, printed in Basle in 1515, with a marginal drawing by Holbein showing Erasmus working at his desk.

depart for war in France, Henry was to have the pretender to the throne, Edmund de la Pole, for seven years a helpless prisoner, brought out of the Tower and executed in order to emphasise the importance of loyalty during the King's absence abroad.

Ruthlessness and total lack of scruple were core elements in the character of Henry VIII. Thomas More was flattered when the King slipped an arm lovingly round his neck and walked up and down his Chelsea garden for an hour, talking and laughing. But More well knew that the cruel, weirdly nervous and unpredictable King, egocentric and self-willed · to an obsessive degree, would change his arm for an axe and whip off More's head in a flash if it 'could win him a castle in France'. And that, of course, proved to be the case, though the cause for which Thomas More's head was to pay the price was worth rather more than a French château.

Still, in 1509, the honeymoon atmosphere – and the money to pay for it – overflowed in superabundance. England danced.

> His Majesty [wrote one observer a year or so later] is the handsomest potentate I ever set eyes on; above the usual height, with an extremely fine calf to his leg, his complexion fair and bright, with auburn hair combed straight and short in the French fashion, and a round face so very beautiful that it would become a pretty woman, his throat being rather long and thick.

This colossus of a Prince was not simply beautiful, he was accomplished too. 'He speaks French, English, Latin and a little Italian; plays well on the lute and harpsichord, sings from the book at sight, draws the bow with greater strength than any man in England, and jousts marvellously.'

'He is . . . a great deal handsomer than the King of France'

Later on, in his twenties, Henry was described as 'extremely handsome. Nature could not have done more for him. He is much handsomer than any other sovereign in Christendom – a great deal handsomer than the King of France, very fair and his whole frame admirably proportioned.' That was one of the most welcome compliments anyone could pay Henry, for if his vanity had an Achilles heel it was his envy of Francis I, the handsome young man who became King of France in January 1515. Henry once showed his muscular calf to the Venetian ambassador and demanded his assurance that Francis could not exhibit anything so handsome and swelling.

His Majesty came into our arbor, and addressing me in French, said 'Talk with me awhile. The King of France is he as tall as I am?' I told him there was but little difference. He continued, 'Is he as stout?' I said he was not; and he then inquired, 'What sort of leg has he?' I replied 'Spare'. Whereupon he opened the front of his doublet, and placing his hand on his thigh, said: 'look here; and I also have a good calf to my leg.'

He then told me he was very fond of this King of France, and that on more than three occasions [in 1513] he was very near him with his army, but that he [Francis] would never allow himself to be seen, and always retreated, which His Majesty attributed to deference for King Louis, who did not choose an engagement to take place.

On hearing that Francis 1 wore a beard, he allowed his own to grow, and as it is reddish, he has now got a beard that looks like gold.

Francis could not boast comparison with so noble a metal – nor could he match Henry's galaxy of talents. 'He [Henry] is very accomplished, a good musician, composes well, is a capital horseman, a fine jouster, speaks French, Latin and Spanish.' Above all he was energetic, brimming over with a sustained *joie de vivre* that was truly prodigious. Few of his courtiers had the stamina to stand the gruelling pace he set, for paying suit to him took on literally the quality of a perpetual point-to-point across the roughest terrain the English countryside could provide.

He is very fond of hunting, and never takes his diversion without tiring eight or ten horses which he causes to be stationed beforehand along the line of country he means to take, and when one is tired he mounts another, and before he gets home they are all exhausted. He is extremely fond of tennis, at which game it is the prettiest thing in the world to see him play, his fair skin glowing through a shirt of the finest texture.

If this emphatic heartiness had been all, Henry would have been a boorish fellow. 'He spares no pains to convert the sport of hunting into a royal martyrdom,' complained one saddle-sore follower. Henry's single-handed tournaments on horse and foot with his favourite jousting companion, the Duke of Suffolk, later to become his brother-in-law, were likened to the combats of Achilles and Hector – but those legendary figures were credited, at least, with a certain spiritual refinement. And so it was with Henry, for along with his open-air high jinks went an intellectual cultivation that was earnest if not remarkably subtle. He applied himself to theology, to the newly fashionable language of ancient Greek, and also to mathematics. Thomas More's son-in-law, William Roper, described how Henry would take the Lord Chancellor

> into his private room, and there some time in matters of astronomy, geometry, divinity and such other faculties, and some time in his worldly affairs, [would] sit and confer with him. And other whiles would he in the night have him up into the leads [the roof] there to consider with the diversities, courses, motions and operation of the stars and planets.

It is rather reminiscent of that other flamboyant royal libertine, Charles II, debating earnestly with the Royal Society on abstruse scientific problems, and, of course, the people of England loved both rascals the more for their serious side. King James I was equally academic but he made the mistake of choosing gay young men as the objects of his private and public favours – rather than Nell Gwynns or Anne Boleyns.

Not that Henry VIII, in the early years of his reign, strayed very far from his marriage bed, for Catherine responded to his youthful vigour with enthusiasm both private and public. After all, on 11 June 1509, her wedding day, she had been the best part of ten years waiting for her prince – Arthur or Henry – to come. And the coronation which followed within a fortnight was remarkable not only for the joy with which England greeted its new King, but for the delighted affection which the King and Queen demonstrated for each other. They were, manifestly, very much in love with each other and this provided a heart-warming touch that happily rounded off the convivial atmosphere in which Henry VIII's reign opened.

The coronation was a magnificent affair processing through streets draped with cloth of gold, with Henry's costume being the most fantastic of a whole collection of bejewelled, elaborate outfits worn by the Court.

> If I should declare [wrote Edward Hall, a chronicler who did not usually flag at the task of describing the minutiae of Tudor ceremonial] what pain, labour and diligence the tailors, embroiderers and goldsmiths took both to make and devise garments for lords, ladies, knights and esquires and also for decking, trapping

and adorning of coursers, jennets and palfreys [all horses] it were too long to rehearse: but for a surety, more rich, nor more strange nor more curious works hath not been seen than were prepared for this coronation.

Rich, strange and curious too were the celebrations that went on for days after the ceremony itself. The wedding feast was 'greater than any Caesar had known' and was opened by a procession, led by the Duke of Buckingham and the Lord Steward on horseback, bearing exotic dishes into the banqueting hall. Then, having gorged themselves, the company staggered

The coronation of Henry VIII in Westminster Abbey, on Midsummer Day, 1509. Drawing from the roll of John Islip, Abbot of Westminster.

outside to enjoy a tournament whose combats went on until dusk.

Henry did not take part himself in the battles – though he could throw a four-yard-long javelin further than most, draw the bow with greater strength and fire it with greater accuracy than any of his contemporaries. It was not for several months, until just after the New Year's celebrations of 1510, that he donned armour to compete in a private joust at Richmond. He was supposed to be fighting incognito, as a mysterious helmeted stranger. It was the sort of charade Henry loved to play. But his opponent, Sir William Compton, a gentleman of the Privy Chamber, must have known whom he was up against, for Henry's size, gait and manner already had a regality all their own, and the occasion was conveniently provided with courtly eye-witnesses. Compton sportingly offered little fight and was, for his pains, struck down by the masked man of mystery who beat him nearly to death. We can assume, though, that Sir William managed at least a polite laugh when the merry jape was officially revealed.

The rounds of merry-making were unceasing. During the summer of 1511 Henry went on a progress and diverted himself 'in shooting, singing, dancing, wrestling, casting of the bar, playing at the recorders, flute and virginals, and in setting of songs, making of ballads and did set two godly Masses, every one of them of five parts, which were sung oftentimes in his chapel and afterwards in divers other places'.

Music was one of Henry's consuming passions, and whatever suspicions one may have about the other talents attributed to him by adoring courtiers, there is no doubt that his musical taste and abilities were of the highest order. The British Museum contains manuscripts of excellent vocal and instrumental compositions, much more certainly his than the usually attributed *Greensleeves*. He could pick out the most intricate melodies on the lute, was no mean hand at the organ and could accompany his own singing on the virginals. His voice was direct and tuneful, and he sang solos or part-songs, reading his own harmony by sight from sheet music. He loved to sing with and to listen to the choirs of his own Chapels Royal, and he and his choirmasters went scouting for talent all over England.

Henry was, indeed, as Dr Scarisbrick has described him, 'the last of the troubadours and the heir of Burgundian chivalry: a youth wholly absorbed in dance and song, courtly love and knight errantry'. He loved to hawk, watching his birds swoop down from the sky to sweep up their prey and then return, to be exotically hooded on his own great jewelled glove. 'His fingers were one mass of jewelled rings,' wrote the Venetian ambassador, 'and around his neck he wore a gold collar from which hung a diamond as big as a walnut.' His clothes were magnificent to match: sumptuous silks, cloth of gold, sarcenets, satins, almost luminously-tinted feathers and, of course, jewels and precious metals sprinkled everywhere.

This all cost money – £335 to a Parisian jeweller, one Jacques Maryn, £566 for a thousand pearls and other jewels, and a constant flow of payments to oil the mechanism of Court festivities: ten shillings for a Midsummer bonfire, ten marks to the 'Lord of Misrule' who presided over the lavish celebrations of the New Year in 1511, and £800 for New Year presents – though much of that last sum would have been recouped from the presents which the King received in return. Henry's bounty was prodigal.

Not content with pouring out his father's cornucopia of carefully garnered wealth at home, the new King decided to spend it even faster abroad and to purchase for himself what every young martial prince most desired, the honours of war. Playing at war in the tiltyard was not enough. It was only eighty years since Henry VI had been crowned King of France in Paris itself. Henry V was a resounding and none-too-distant legend – indeed, Henry VIII probably saw himself as the true heir to the victor of Agincourt. He commissioned a translation of Titus Livius's life of Henry V and the translator, predictably and perhaps even to cue, called upon the latest Henry to emulate the exploits of the old. War was still, after all, the *raison d'être* of the feudal hierarchy which shaped English society, and the upper classes held their eminence precisely because they could command the resources, and had the ability, to fight.

The new King lost no time in making plain where his intentions lay. One of his accession declarations was to wage war against Louis XII, whose gout-ridden semi-senility apparently annoyed Henry to the same degree that the martial youth of Francis, Louis's nephew and successor, was later to

'A youth wholly absorbed in dance and song, courtly love and knight errantry'

25

Henry VIII: Musical Virtuoso

Henry was a great patron of music. He brought over from the Continent many master musicians, Philip van Wilder, the great Dutch lute-player, de Opitiis, the Italian organist, and, most famous of all, Dionisio Memo, the celebrated organist of St Mark's Cathedral in Venice.

Henry gathered around himself a band of minstrels, who accompanied him on his travels both in England and abroad. He also amassed a collection of peerless musical instruments – lutes, trumpets, viols, rebecs, sackbuts, drums, harpsichords and organs.

ABOVE RIGHT Illustrated page from Henry VIII's own psalter, showing musicians from the Court playing pipe and tabor, trumpet, harp and clavichord.

RIGHT The music for one of Henry's own compositions – the song 'Pastance with good company' (Pastime with good company).

LEFT Detail from the ceiling of the Chapel Royal at Hampton Court, showing one of the pendants decorated by angels blowing wind instruments.

BELOW Page from a sixteenth-century manuscript writing book, with calligraphic and decorative tablets.

excite his envy. He gratuitously insulted a French envoy come to congratulate him on his accession, and then swaggered out, pointedly, to a mock war being held in the tiltyard. He also wrote secretly to his father-in-law, Ferdinand of Spain, to investigate the possibility of a two-pronged attack on France.

But Henry had to wait three years before English chargers could canter over the lilies of France, for he had inherited a Council which had ruled England with his father 'without sword and bloodshed' and which could not all be dealt with like Empson and Dudley: there was Warham, the Chancellor and the Archbishop of Canterbury, who had married Henry to Catherine and crowned them both; Fox, Bishop of Winchester and Lord Privy Seal, who had baptised Henry; Fisher, the ascetic Bishop of Rochester, who had preached Henry VII's funeral oration; and Ruthal, the Bishop of Durham. The young King sat uneasily among these venerable clerics and left much of the day-to-day business of State to them.

They sent off, shortly after his accession, and in his name, a routine expression of peace and goodwill to the King of France.

Henry walking in procession to Parliament in 1512. He is accompanied by his temporal lords, whose names and armorial bearings appear above their representations.

When a French envoy returned the compliment, Henry exploded. 'Who wrote this letter?' he cried. 'I ask peace of the King of France? – who dare not look at me, let alone make war?' Late in 1509 Henry despatched Christopher Bainbridge, the Archbishop of York and the only prelate in favour of a war policy, to confer with the warrior Pope Julius II and to organise an alliance against France. Warham, Fox, Fisher and Ruthal, in the meantime, hurried through a friendship treaty *with* the French, and tried to slow down Henry's attempts to get closely involved with his father-in-law, Ferdinand of Spain.

In fact, it was Ferdinand who called the tune. He was very keen to use his wealthy and energetic young son-in-law to further his own, Spanish, designs against France, but in 1509 and 1510 the moment was not propitious. In the meantime, on New Year's Day 1511, Queen Catherine was safely delivered of a son, an apparently healthy little boy. Henry was transported with delight. The tournament and pageant he gave to celebrate the birth of an heir rivalled the lavishness of the coronation festivities. He had his clothes embroidered with great 'Hs' and

Henry jousting before Catherine of Aragon at the tournament held on 12 February 1512 to celebrate the birth of Henry, Prince of Wales, who lived for less than two months. The initial 'K' for Catherine and the motto 'Coure loyall' (True heart) are embroidered upon Henry's surcoat and upon the trappings of his horse. Illustration from the Great Tournament Roll of Westminster.

'Ks' in pure gold thread and, as an orgiastic variation on the normal system of distributing charity on such occasions, allowed the crowds to rip them off his back, bellowing and guffawing the while. The boy was christened Henry and named Prince of Wales, but then suddenly, less than two months old, he mysteriously died.

Henry was heartbroken, but there was some consolation. For by the middle of 1511 both Ferdinand and the Pope had become disenchanted with the League of Cambrai, the alliance they had formed with France to rape the republic of Venice. Venice had submitted, but France had had all the pleasure – and profit – while Ferdinand and the Pope watched impotent on the sidelines. Through Bainbridge in Rome and, in London, through Catherine, for she was effectively her father's ambassador, Henry was invited to join a Holy Alliance which would set upon France and, hopefully, yield the most unholy profits for the adventurers concerned. The Pope hoped, of course, to get at least his fair share of the Venetian spoils. Spain hoped to annex for herself the kingdom of Navarre. And

30

England hoped for glory and restoration of some part of the empire which, until Joan of Arc's crusade, had stretched south of the Loire, but which now comprised simply the French port of Calais.

Suddenly turned upon by their former allies, the French were understandably upset. Louis XII, particularly put out by the Pope's *volte-face* which he justifiably described 'as a dagger plunged through the heart', promptly lined up behind him the patriotic French Church, ever ready to take offence at Rome's 'interference' in French ecclesiastical affairs. A council of French cardinals and bishops declared itself willing, in the last resort, to depose the Pope. It was a fair tit for tat, but it also made it very difficult for the clerics on the English Council to resist their King's desire to start his armies marching. The French were flouting the ordained powers of the Holy Father. Henry's martial ambitions had suddenly been sanctified. And so, bitterly denouncing the 'cruel, impious, criminal and un-speakable' French attempt to 'lacerate the seamless garment of Christ' and to 'destroy the unity of the church', Henry VIII led his nation into a Holy War.

It was a disaster. In June 1512 the Marquess of Dorset sailed out of Southampton Water bound for Gascony with twelve thousand men. They reached the port of Fuentarrabia, intending, with the help of the Spanish, to attack Bayonne. But the Spanish never showed up. While France was concentrating on rebuffing an English attack, Ferdinand sent his troops into Navarre, occupied it thoroughly and declared the campaign at an end. He had got what he wanted and, to forestall any complaints, bitterly criticised the English force, which had mutinied and sailed home without waiting for orders, bankrupt and diseased after four months' pointless waiting. Ferdinand's treachery was transparent, but so mortified was Henry by his army's collapse that he accepted his father-in-law's strictures and not only upbraided his officers in the presence of the Council and the Spanish ambassador, but asked the Spaniards to suggest a suit-able punishment. The surprised but scornful suggestion was, of course, none at all.

Humiliated, Henry planned a campaign for the following spring that he himself would lead. English envoys persuaded the Holy Roman Emperor Maximilian to join the Holy Alliance

The armour for Henry VIII and his horse. Around the hem of the King's skirt are the initials 'H' and 'K', linked by true lovers' knots. The armour was made for Henry at Greenwich by Flemish and Italian craftsmen. It is now in the Tower of London.

and so it was that in March 1513, France seemed faced with the prospect of a vast, four-pronged attack. But Ferdinand proved true to his character, if to nothing else. He went behind his allies' backs to conclude a secret truce with Louis XII that left him in peaceful possession of Navarre, and then coolly deserted his son-in-law. He simply shrugged off the remonstrances of Henry, on whom, nevertheless, the light was finally, slowly dawning. For the English plan of campaign had been shaped so as to be independent of any Spanish co-operation – a direct attack in the traditional fashion on northern France from England's only bridgehead, Calais.

On a fine Midsummer evening, at 7 p.m. on 30 June 1513,

with the setting sun glinting glamorously on his armour, the King of England set foot on his sole remaining Continental possession. After three weeks of pageantry – symbolic representation of the glories to come – the English army lumbered off inland at the rate of three miles a day. Its first bivouac, on 21 July 1513, was soaked with rain, but true to the example of Henry V, the King refused to take off his sodden garments but rode round the camp to inspire his drenched men. Doubtless they appreciated the gesture and, encouraged also by a spell of decent weather, they speeded up their march to reach the town of Thérouanne, forty miles off, in eleven days.

It was no accident that, on 1 August 1513, Henry VIII set about besieging Thérouanne's walls with vigour, for this was the town captured by Edward III after Crécy. Maximilian, the Emperor, arrived as had been pre-arranged, and skilfully allayed Henry's dismay at the small size of the army he had brought by offering to fight not as Henry's ally but as a subordinate general. The Imperial forces would fight under the English flag. The fact that Henry would have to pay them as well did not in the slightest diminish the English King's pleasure at lording it over the Holy Roman Emperor.

A fortnight later the English forces won the glory that Henry had invested so much of father's money to capture. On 16 August 1513 a group of French cavalry misjudged its position, turned tail and fled, but left to be captured and ransomed an expensive and prestigious collection of noblemen which included a duke, a marquis and the vice-admiral of France. In fact, the title given to the skirmish, the Battle of the Spurs, precisely described the only dangerous weapon the French brandished in the English soldiers' faces as they galloped helter-skelter over the horizon, but Henry announced that his forces had won a major victory – and the Emperor Maximilian did not disagree. When Thérouanne fell on 24 August he received the town as a gift from Henry, and promptly had it razed to the ground.

This sharp punishment for excessive resistance was the principal reason why, one month later, the town of Tournai surrendered after only eight days' siege. And Henry decided that this fine fortified citadel, the seat of a bishop, should be spared to become a second Calais. He spent three weeks

The embarkation of the King and his Court at Dover,
as they prepared to cross to Boulogne in 1520.
Henry can be seen on the second ship to the right.

34

Autograph letter from Catherine of Aragon to Henry in France, giving news of the Battle of Flodden. The Queen had been made Governor of the realm and Captain-General of the armed forces in Henry's absence.

celebrating this splendid doubling of his Continental empire in the ostentatious and mock-violent fashion of jousts and tournaments which Europe now acknowledged as his own hallmark. And then he returned home, well-pleased with himself.

Much had happened in his absence. In August James IV of Scotland, prizing Scotland's 'auld alliance' with France above the marriage which made him Henry VIII's brother-in-law, had led his armies over the Tweed. Thomas Howard, Earl of Surrey, took a smaller English force north to meet him at Flodden Edge, between Berwick and the Cheviots, and in three hours' ferocious fighting there destroyed the Scots completely. On the evening of 9 September 1513 ten thousand Scots lay dead on Flodden field – most of the aristocracy, a dozen earls, three bishops and King James himself. It took Scotland a quarter of a century to recover. Indeed, if Henry had not wasted so much time jousting in Tournai he could that autumn have seized control of his sister Margaret, her baby son, now James V, and the whole of Scotland. But his eyes were set on Europe. He had plans for another, yet more glorious Continental campaign in 1514. The Pope had secretly promised and shown to Bainbridge in Rome a document confirming sanctified sovereignty for Henry over the whole of France and, indeed, the Crown of France, if Henry could physically win possession of them for himself. The Pope might even, it was hinted, travel to Paris personally to place the French crown on the English King's head.

It was a glittering prospect for a young man not five years on the throne of England. Yet it came to nothing. There were all sorts of circumstantial difficulties, and certain very obvious practical obstacles to the realisation of the dream. But the principal reason why, in 1514, the story of Henry VIII and English history swung in another direction was because of the personal intervention of a man who had been Henry's almoner during the French campaign. Ambitious, vain and greedy, but inordinately hard-working and intelligent, this cleric had organised the complex logistics of keeping the English army fed, healthy and disciplined with remarkable skill and efficiency. He had won Henry's affection with a basic, earthy humour and boisterous tastes that contrasted strangely with his administrative competence, and he had been rewarded with the bishopric of the fine double-ringed and turreted town of Tournai. He was within months to become the effective ruler of Henry VIII's England and, within years, aspired to rule all of Christendom by becoming Pope. Some forty years old, he was the son of a butcher and cattle-dealer of Ipswich, and his name was Thomas Wolsey.

2 To whiche Court?
1514-20

THERE WERE THOSE in sixteenth-century England, and this shows just how little the Renaissance really was an age of universal reason and modern learning, who seriously believed that the relationship between Henry VIII and Thomas Wolsey was based on witchcraft. The two men who jointly ruled England for fifteen years seemed sinisterly kindred spirits.

There was a physical resemblance, for a start. Wolsey was a gross, corpulent fellow, and Henry turned into the same figure of a man as, over the years, he lost his lithe youthfulness. More significant – for Henry's corporation did not flower into its full, bloated glory until after Wolsey's death – they shared the same style of life. Both were greedy creatures of the flesh, extroverted, ostentatious, astonishingly ambitious, ruthless and unscrupulous, indifferent to the shame ordinary mortals attach to certain mean and cruel acts.

Yet their animal tastes aside, Henry VIII and Wolsey were both highly intelligent and extremely industrious men, and it was from the division of their gigantic energies that their working relationship sprang. For though no one could accuse Henry of being a sluggard, he did not like real work. His idea of a King's day involved rising early, going out with the hounds, hawking, jousting or playing tennis, presiding over the pageantry of his Court, dancing, dicing, masquing and banqueting. And into this strenuous routine he threw himself with enthusiasm and unstinting effort. There was little room for the tedious details of letter signing and proclamation drafting, haggling with foreign emissaries or keeping operational the military and courtly apparatus which Henry needed to display himself as every inch a King. And this became Wolsey's responsibility, indeed, his *raison d'être*. For when in the early years of the reign old Warham and Fox had acted like a couple of schoolmasters, nagging Henry to spend more time at the Council table, it was the youthful King's almoner who had urged otherwise. The more the bishops scolded Henry to apply himself, the more 'busily did the almoner persuade him to the contrary: which delighted him so much and caused him to have greater affection and love for the almoner … Who was now in high favour, but Master Almoner? And who ruled all under the King, but Master Almoner?'

Wolsey had worked conscientiously to reach the eminence

CARDINAL   WOLSE

Cardinal Wolsey, portrait
by an unknown artist.

he had attained by 1514. A clever schoolboy, he had pursued
one of the few roads to advancement open to the son of humble
parents – a career in the Church. He went up to Oxford, took
his BA at around the usual age – fifteen – but had shown such
promise that he was made a fellow, then bursar of Magdalen. He
became chaplain to Archbishop Deane, Warham's predecessor
at Canterbury, and reached Court in 1507, in his mid-thirties,
as chaplain to Henry VII. The accession of Henry VIII gave
Wolsey not only a seat on the Council but the position of
almoner, which involved personal dealings with the King. By

1514, after his season in France as Henry's aide-de-camp, Wolsey was effectively controlling access to the royal presence – though his sudden rise was not, as has sometimes been asserted, to the great annoyance of the Councillors he displaced. Warham and Fox both seem, initially at least, to have regarded the energetic Thomas as something of a protégé, and they used him as a pack-horse onto whom they could load the cares of State that had been burdening them too long. Fox, indeed, seems to have felt positively guilty about all the worries and responsibility he shuffled off onto Wolsey, urging him not to work after six o'clock in the evening. The two bishops went back gratefully to their dioceses, leaving Wolsey to manage the exuberant monarch who had proved somewhat more than they could cope with.

Wolsey coped by giving Henry exactly what he wanted. If some new alliance or agreement were being mooted, Wolsey would not trouble the King with every clause. He simply sent a digest or 'extracts' because 'it should be painful for your grace to read the whole treaty'. If Henry wanted to write personally to someone he asked Wolsey to prepare a draft that he could simply copy out – but that was rare.

The two men understood each other, and, for a long time, liked each other well, and this is the more remarkable since their relationship was, for much of the time, an impersonal matter of letters and notes carried by shuttle service between Wolsey in London and the King wherever he might be hunting or visiting. It made for long delays, especially as, even when Henry received the despatches, he left them for days unopened or unsigned while banquets, horses or hawks consumed his interest.

Illustration from the biography of Wolsey, written by his servant George Cavendish. The scene shown here depicts Wolsey travelling by barge to the royal palace at Greenwich. (Bodleian Ms. Douce 363 folio 58).

Wolsey became a man of magnificence: Archbishop of York in 1514, Cardinal and Chancellor in 1515, Papal Legate in 1518. The grandiose palaces he built were literally fit for a King, as Henry rapidly demonstrated when he cut Wolsey down in 1529, taking over Hampton Court, which Wolsey had begun in 1515, and incorporating York Palace into his new palace of Whitehall. Foreigners assumed that Wolsey was King in all but name, and scurrilous little rhymes circulated:

> Why come ye not to court?
> To whiche court?
> To the Kinges court
> Or to Hampton Court?
>
> (JOHN SKELTON)

But Henry never totally abdicated the running of the realm, as ambassadors who were suddenly set upon by Henry, having their gracious proposals slashed through for the self-serving contrivances they were, came to realise. Wolsey could be overruled and the flaws in his plans laid bare by a royal intervention, which might be rare, but seldom failed to grasp a problem firmly by the scruff of the neck. And there can be no doubt that the great achievements of the period, the events that have made Henry VIII's reign one of the most decisive and formative in English history – his first divorce, the break with Rome and the creation of a new, dynamic autocratic monarchy – all these stemmed directly, and solely, from Henry himself.

Still, for over a dozen years, Henry left to Thomas Wolsey the day-to-day running of English affairs, and such were the priorities of both King and Cardinal that for much of the time this meant foreign affairs. Domestic responsibilities were either ignored or scornfully flouted. Parliaments (called in 1510, 1512, 1515 and 1523) were methods of raising money for foreign adventures. One can, indeed, almost date Henry's wars from the years when he deigned to call Parliament, and the Church was treated with equal casualness. Wolsey regarded it simply as the mechanism by which he maintained his European eminence, the source of his titles, dignity and wealth. Spiritual or pastoral care did not figure prominently on his list of priorities. He always held at least one other bishopric in addition to York – and never visited the seats of any of them. Though not a monastic priest, he held the abbey of St Albans for the sake of its wealth. He openly sold bishoprics and promotion to the highest bidder. And, despite his vows of chastity and celibacy, he not only fathered a son, but bestowed upon the infant some most valuable benefices.

It is probably true that, during the period when Wolsey was Chancellor and took an interest in the law courts, the poor got good justice, but this was, again, a reflection of the Cardinal's pride rather than his humanity. He sat in judgment in the Star Chamber, by-passing ordinary Common Law and hearing cases with such ceremony and authority that it seemed to some contemporaries – and to some historians since – that he must have invented some sort of special court. In fact, he was sitting 'in Star Chamber' as a member of the Privy Council in its long established judicial function, hearing cases brought directly by subjects who felt they could get no justice from the ordinary courts of the land. In later years the Council, sitting in the famous chamber with the multi-starred ceiling, did take on a certain administrative independence, but under Wolsey it was simply the style of the man that appeared to lend it an existence and glory of its own. Many petitioners benefited from the autocratic impartiality of his decisions, but that was an indirect benefit they were lucky to get from Wolsey's delight in power. After all, one of the most king-like things that he, a commoner, could do was to dispense justice like some latter-day Solomon to the poor and needy. Foreign ambassadors were most impressed, and it was the respect of Europe that Wolsey courted, not affection nearer home.

Within months of gaining the King's ear, Wolsey had pulled off his first *coup*. Henry had returned from Tournai thirsting for a second, more ambitious, campaign against France in 1514. Ferdinand of Spain and the Emperor Maximilian were to join in the triple attack. But both Ferdinand and Maxmilian, true to form, played false. They concluded secret treaties with France, leaving Henry alone to launch the offensive, from which they had nothing to lose and much, if it proved successful, to gain. They must have been very pleased with themselves.

But there was a new hand guiding England through the treacherous waters of Continental diplomacy, and Wolsey was more than a match for Ferdinand and Maximilian. He saw that the two double-dealers had overreached themselves. They had in recent years been so successful in avoiding real confrontation with France, that Louis XII was no longer afraid of them. He knew he could buy them off. It was Henry, in no need of French blood money, patently pugnacious and possessing armies which had in 1513 triumphed at Thérouanne, Tournai and Flodden, who was the real menace. So Wolsey got good terms when, in a sudden *volte-face*, he accepted France's peace initiative – possession of Tournai, a handsome amount of French gold, and marriage between Mary, Henry's sister, and Louis XII.

Henry was delighted with the *coup* and the man who had helped him achieve it. Within months Wolsey was wearing a Cardinal's hat and Chancellor's gown. Henry was particularly pleased, because his French alliance gave him a weapon he could turn against his treacherous father-in-law. He now made no secret of what he thought of Ferdinand. The wretched Spanish ambassador had to put up with so many wounding insults that he complained he was simply 'a bull, at whom everyone throws darts'. And, though Catherine was pregnant again, there was even some talk of a divorce.

Henry sent over to France to plot an attack on Spain Charles Brandon, the drinking and jousting companion he had raised from being a commoner to the dukedom of Suffolk. He was a hearty, handsome fellow, claimed as a husband by three women and enviously adored for his amorous achievements by Henry who was still a faithful, if increasingly restive, spouse. Whenever Henry enjoyed himself, Suffolk was there, hunting, jousting, dancing. Indeed, he saw far more of the King than did Wolsey, so it was said that Henry divided up England between the 'two obstinate men that governed everything'. Yet Suffolk's friendship with the King never at this time threatened Wolsey's power, and his trip to France in 1514 closed a chapter in whatever immediate political ambitions he may have had. For, as a cover to his mission to plot Ferdinand's destruction, he was supposed to act as Henry's representative at the marriage and coronation in France of Mary Tudor, generally supervising the welfare of the English King's beautiful young sister.

He played the part too well. Mary, then eighteen, was one of the ikons of the age. 'A nymph from heaven ... a paradise' said the Venetian ambassador. There had been a public outcry against her proposed marriage to the toothless old Louis XII,

OVERLEAF The Field of the Cloth of Gold, the meeting place of Henry and Francis I of France in June 1520. In the left foreground, Henry and Cardinal Wolsey are shown arriving in procession, and at the top of the picture, the two sovereigns meet.

Omine fa paiz entre dieu et les homes.
Par le moyen de la Vierge marie.
ffut iadis faicte ainfy a prefent foirne.
Bourgois francoys defchinez de nos fomes.
Car marie auecq nous fe marie.

The marriage of Louis XII of France and Mary Tudor, Henry's younger sister, in 1514. This illustration was executed by Pierre Gringoire, an eye-witness at the wedding ceremony.

and Mary had consented to the match only when Henry promised her that she could marry the lover of her choice when Louis died – which occurred within eleven weeks of the marriage.

Mary was free, not simply of her husband but also, through her brother's promise, of the obligations that conventionally bound princesses to sacrifice their passions on the altar of diplomacy. Louis's lascivious nephew and successor Francis I, however, had other ideas. His uncle was scarcely cold when, every evening, he forced his attentions upon the beautiful widow whom Suffolk, by now, felt a more than patriotic duty

Detail from the portrait
of Charles v, Holy Roman
Emperor and King of
Spain, by Van Orly.

to protect. Francis was 'importunate with her in divers matters not to her honour', wrote Suffolk indignantly to Henry.

A more serious threat was the possibility that Henry might go back on his word and marry off his sister to the nephew of Catherine of Aragon, the Archduke Charles, who was shortly to succeed to the possessions of both the Emperor Maximilian and Ferdinand. Charles was the grandson of both and owed to generations of in-breeding not only his enormous double inheritance but also his jutting, graceless Habsburg chin. He might be about to become the most powerful ruler in Europe but he seemed to Mary to be definitely the ugliest. She was aghast at the prospect. 'I would rather be torn in pieces,' she stoutly declared, in an episode which Professor Pollard, the great chronicler of these years, has incomparably depicted:

> Suffolk tried in vain to soothe her fears. She refused to listen and brought him to his knees with the announcement that unless he would wed her there and then, she would continue to believe that he had only come to entice her back to England and force her into marriage with Charles. What was the poor Duke to do, between his promise to Henry and the pleading of Mary? He did what every other man with a heart in his breast and warm blood in his veins would have done, he cast prudence to the winds and secretly married the woman he loved.

Henry, of course, was furious, as he often was when anyone took him at his word. In later years Suffolk's head would have rolled. But Mary was Henry's favourite sister. He had grown up, one suspects, a little under the thumb of Margaret, his tough elder sister who had married the King of Scotland, and, against the rules of succession, his Will was to place Mary's offspring above Margaret's in line of title to the throne. Mary and Suffolk were forgiven. By the time the two lovers apprehensively reached England, the royal wrath had cooled and their clandestine liaison was publicly solemnised at Greenwich on 13 May 1515 in the presence of Henry and the entire Court. Wolsey was probably distressed that Mary could no longer serve as a pawn in his European designs, but her marriage did mean that the Suffolks would have to live away from Court, for though their indiscretion was forgiven, it could not be too openly flaunted. Henry would hunt with less substantial companions, and the Cardinal alone would have the King's ear.

OPPOSITE Wedding
portrait of Mary Tudor,
Dowager Queen of France,
and Charles Brandon,
Duke of Suffolk, 1515.
Fortunately for the couple,
Mary was Henry's
favourite sister, and
Charles his closest
companion, so that the
King forgave them for
marrying without his
consent, and welcomed
them back to Court.

ABOVE Antoine Macault
presenting his translation
of Diodorus of Sicily to
Francis I, who is shown
surrounded by his children
and his Court.

The only problem of the whole episode was the role played
in it by this new French King, Francis I. Once his lascivious
proposals had been stamped on, Francis had done everything in
his power to hasten the young lovers' union and, of course, to
frustrate the possibility of a marriage alliance between England
and the Habsburg heir. To that extent, the marriage had played
right into his hands. And Francis provided Henry with many
other causes of irritation. Twenty years old, of a military ability
which he soon demonstrated, and good looks which were
described, literally, as devilishly attractive, the French King
replaced Henry as Christendom's rising star. 'Francis', wrote
the Bishop of Worcester, 'is tall in stature, broad-shouldered,
oval and handsome in face, very slender in the legs and much
inclined to corpulence.' He sounded like a mirror image of
Henry.

This rival aroused not only Henry's envy, but also his suspicions, for that very summer Francis despatched from his Court to Scotland, John Stuart, Duke of Albany. Albany was a prince of the blood royal and heir presumptive to the Scottish throne and, capitalising on the distrust the Scots felt for Margaret Tudor, who was acting as Regent for her infant son James v, he seized control of the young King and sent Margaret packing. She was driven to take refuge at the Court of her brother, who was already inflamed with envy by Francis's brilliant military achievements. The French armies had marched into Italy, sweeping all before them and, on 13 September 1515 at Marignano, convincingly overwhelmed the Swiss and Milanese in the 'Battle of the Giants' which gave Francis control of all northern Italy. The Pope had no choice but to let him have Milan, and Rome itself became, effectively, a French vassal. Henry had seriously believed himself to be the arbiter of Europe. 'If I choose he will cross the Alps,' he had boasted, 'and if I choose he will not.' Francis, however, had swiftly deflated those pretensions.

Wolsey's solution was not to fight. The Scottish situation meant that Henry was as vulnerable to a stab in the back as he had supposed Francis to be. The Cardinal, instead, offered to subsidise both the Emperor Maximilian and the Swiss if they would take up arms against France. Both accepted the proposition and the money – Henry had practically bankrupted his father's treasury in his seven years of extravagant rule – but neither took up arms with any seriousness. At the beginning of 1516 they marched boldly into Italy, and marched boldly back at the first sign of resistance.

Meanwhile, in January 1516, Ferdinand of Spain, enthusiastically supporting Henry's plan for a pan-European alliance against France, dealt one last crooked hand to his English son-in-law. He died, and to the throne of Spain succeeded the Archduke Charles, who was more than delighted promptly to desert Henry and to conclude a treaty of friendship with Francis. At Noyon Spain professed every good will towards France, and the Emperor Maximilian, Charles's grandfather, was invited to join in the reconciliation – a possibility which sent cold shivers down the spines of Wolsey and Henry. More wagon trains of English money were despatched to keep the Emperor on their

Margaret Tudor, Queen of
Scots, Henry's elder sister.

side. Maximilian received them graciously. '*Mon fils*,' he
chuckled to Charles, '*vous allez tromper les Français, et moi je
vais tromper les Anglais*.' ('My son, you are going to cheat the
French, and I am going to cheat the English'.) In the spring of
1517 he joined the signatories of Noyon. England was – with
scarcely concealed contempt – left out in the cold.

Wolsey's only hope lay in the first part of Maximilian's
aphorism, for Charles, in fact, did not intend to remain eternally
true to France. And realising this, Francis also began putting out
feelers towards England. So suddenly, from being disregarded

53

objects of ridicule, Henry and Wolsey became centres of European attention.

Perhaps the most amazing spectacle in all these years of fevered and complex diplomacy, was the one that took place in St Paul's Cathedral on 3 October 1518. There Cardinal Wolsey sang a glorious High Mass, while in front of him knelt the King of England, all the lay and spiritual peers of England and representatives of the Pope and every major European power, all giving thanks to God for the Universal and Eternal Christian Alliance for International Peace which had just been signed, and which took its name from the city which had made it all possible, London. Henry VIII was, of course, delighted. His attempts to become Europe's arbiter through war had failed. Through peace he had apparently triumphed. After the High Mass he entertained Europe's assembled representatives to the most lavish banquet. And Wolsey, of course, was equally triumphant.

Even the old clerics, who had not approved of all the turns Wolsey's policy had taken since they had handed over power to him, could scarce forbear to cheer. 'It was the best deed that ever was done for England', said Fox to the Cardinal, 'and, next to the King, the praise of it is due to you.' Said a somewhat jaundiced Venetian: 'nothing pleases him [Wolsey] more than to be called the arbiter of Christendom.' The treaty was a feather in the Cardinal's hat of this Englishman who felt himself qualified to become Pope.

Events had, in truth, played into Wolsey's hands. Eighteen months before the signature of his glorious international peace, the Emperor Maximilian had been poleaxed by a stroke. He obviously had little time to live, and, though Charles was expected to inherit his title, the Holy Roman Empire's constitution meant he could only do this through an election – in which Francis I determined to oppose him. If the King of Spain could stand for the Imperial title, so could the King of France. So the two rival princes were well-disposed towards setting aside for several years the danger of military expenditure. Buying the Princes who elected the Holy Roman Emperor was a costly business. The Treaty of London was for them but a clearing of the decks, a preliminary to the sparrings of the Imperial election of 1519, and those sparrings were but the

'The arbiter of Christendom'

54

preliminaries to full-scale war between the two great princes who divided Europe between them. Henry and Wolsey had been at the centre of events when the treaty was signed. But once the election got under way the following year they felt so excluded that they even toyed with the idea of setting Henry up as a third candidate. And once Charles had been elected, sandwiching Francis between Spain and the Imperial client states which stretched from the Netherlands down to northern Italy, England became, very obviously, the moderate make-weight she had always been – though even in this modest role, Henry VIII was to succeed in staging the most gorgeously magnificent event of his entire reign – a reign which was already richly endowed with more than a few extravagant occasions.

One of the clauses which had marked the signing of Wolsey's great treaty of universal peace had been a declaration by Henry and Francis to sink their past differences and to meet personally in the following year, 1519. But the Imperial election had intervened. As a token of good will Henry swore he would not shave until the two monarchs met. He rather fancied himself full-bearded; and, not to be outdone, Francis also foreswore the razor. Unfortunately, the fascinating prospect of the Kings of England and France greeting each other like straggling desert island castaways was frustrated by Queen Catherine, who did not like her husband too bristly. It was a token of the power of her personality, and the enduring affection Henry still felt for her after over ten years of heir-less marriage, that she had her way. She 'daily made him great instance and desired him to put it off for her sake'. The razor was sharpened and the *entente cordiale* chilled noticeably – until it was decided that the love between Henry and Francis was 'not in the beards but in the hearts'.

Plans for the historic embracing of two of Europe's oldest enemies went ahead under the efficient stage-management of Wolsey. And the Cardinal contrived to lay on two extra little occasions, one before and one after, to enhance still further the magnificence of the encounter. The newly-elected Emperor Charles was due, in the summer of 1520, to travel from his Spanish dominions up to his Netherlands possessions. Wolsey suggested that he should call in on Henry on his way up the Channel, and Charles, most apprehensive at the new-found love between France and England, was very glad of the chance to have a preliminary word in Henry's ear. He could then travel on to the Netherlands and meet Henry again after the Anglo-French reunion to try to discover if any schemes hostile to himself had been hatched.

So it was that on 26 May 1520 the Imperial fleet anchored in Dover harbour. Wolsey was rowed out to meet Charles and brought him ashore to Dover Castle. Very late that night Henry arrived at the gallop from London, jumped off his horse and rushed straight into the Emperor's bedroom. The two travel-weary rulers embraced each other with every expression of affection, then rode next day to Canterbury for holy blessing of their encounter. There Charles met, for the first time, his aunt Catherine whose marital problems were, within a few years, to cause him such trouble. The few days that followed were marked by serious discussions, for all the paraphernalia of pageantry were packed up ready for the trip to France. That certainly did not offend the austere Charles, however, who declined the opportunities that Henry did offer him to dance.

After wide-ranging, but hardly conclusive talks and expressions of goodwill, the Emperor re-embarked at Sandwich, where his fleet was waiting. They had sailed up the Channel from Dover, for that harbour was by now seething with the entire English Court and many of the nobility. The upper crust of Tudor society, male and female, one entire social class, was being shipped bodily across the Channel with as many of its servants, followers and flamboyant portable possessions as could be transported. As a total reciprocal gesture it has never been paralleled in history, for in France a similar multitude, the flower of the nation, was moving slowly towards a shallow dip in the land between Guisnes and Ardres, the Val d'Or, carefully chosen by commissioners of both countries as the site of the meeting known ever since as the Field of the Cloth of Gold.

Henry and Catherine were attended by some five thousand followers, decked out in the most sumptuous velvets, satin and cloth of gold. Six thousand workmen were already at work preparing the little city of gaily-coloured tents and pavilions where the English host would camp, and two thousand masons, carpenters and glaziers were labouring hard to convert Guisnes Castle and to erect beside it a special summer palace of almost mythical glory. Food for the thousands of horses and riders had been crossing the Channel for days, with chestfuls of cutlery, crockery and glass. Whatever Wolsey's achievements as a diplomatist, no one can deny him the title of the greatest picnic-stager ever. He worried over every detail, and got it right, from 700 conger eels, 2,014 sheep, 26 dozen heron and 4 bushels of mustard down to £1.0.10d worth of cream for the King's cakes.

In Calais wine flowed free in the streets. Messengers scurried to and fro to synchronise precisely the time of encounter. By 5 June Henry was approaching Guisnes, the very edge of England's territory in France, and Francis was just over the other side of the border at Ardres, where his workmen, less efficient than Wolsey's, had erected a high royal pavilion which collapsed in the wind. On Corpus Christi Day, 7 June 1520, cannon sounded on both sides to signal to the other the moment of their King's departure. Francis was first to reach the Val d'Or. When Henry and his entourage reached the lip of the little valley, the French King and his company were drawn up, tensely silent, at the head of the opposite slope.

It was a dramatic, almost dangerous moment. It looked like a battle array, and both sides had, in fact, feared an ambush from the other. The meeting was intended to symbolise reconciliation after centuries of mutual hatred, mistrust and contempt – and those feelings were very much alive on that

Drawing of tents for Henry's encampment at the Field of the Cloth of Gold.

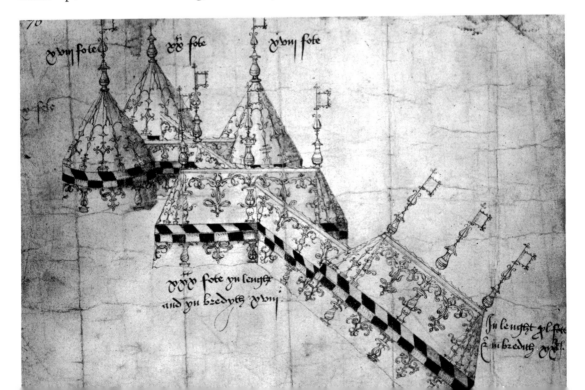

The meeting of Henry and Francis at the Field of the Cloth of Gold, from a stone monument at Rouen.

summer's day. The *raison d'être* of the group of nobles surrounding each king was to wage war on the other. The monarchs themselves had cultivated an almost vicious rivalry between each other. Both were capable of being arrogant, pig-headed and vindictive, anything but angels of light and peace.

Yet now, when the trumpets sounded, Henry and Francis rode down their little slopes towards each other, to a point marked by a spear in the ground. Still in the saddle, they embraced each other, then they dismounted and embraced each other again. For two whole weeks French and English danced together and sang. They jousted every day but one, when the wind was too high, and then they wrestled. This was the famous moment, recorded in all the French chronicles but in none of the English, when Francis threw Henry flat on his broad regal back. Yet even that temporary humiliation did not disturb the flow of friendly reconciliation, smoothly presided over by Wolsey, the crimson satin-clothed Master of Ceremon-

ies, who rode humbly on a mule, as befitted a man of God, and was escorted by two hundred crimson velvet-clad gentlemen and two hundred crimson-dressed archers, as befitted an arbiter of State. The mule too, of course, was dressed in crimson velvet, and all her trappings were of gold.

Eye-witnesses called the Field of the Cloth of Gold the eighth wonder of the world, and certainly, when, at the end of it all, the great Cardinal sang High Mass to the assembled Kings and Courts some real human achievement seemed to have been purchased by all the folly and extravagance. It was graciously symbolic that the two royal choirs should not only sing in harmony, but that their organists, specially transported to this open meadow in northern France, should accompany the *other's* choir and not their own. Where music mingled, how could hearts remain hardened and apart? Before they separated, King Henry VIII and King Francis I vowed solemnly that they would together build a chapel to Our Lady of Peace on the spot where they had embraced and loved each other so heartily.

3 The King's Great Matter 1520-8

OUR LADY OF PEACE did not, unfortunately, get her chapel, for within two years England and France were at war. Henry VIII went directly from the Field of the Cloth of Gold to meet the Emperor Charles. Late in 1521 the King and Emperor signed a treaty of common cause against France. And in 1522 the Earl of Surrey was leading armed English raiders over the same green pastures in which they had embraced France's nobles – and a few of France's ladies – as sworn bosom friends.

War between Francis and Charles had been inevitable long before the junketings of 1520. The trouble was that Francis had little to offer England, whereas Charles could tempt Henry with the prospect of as much French territory as his armies could devour – and Wolsey with the glitter of the Papal tiara. So England deserted France and lined up with the Emperor, until in 1525 Charles not only defeated Francis but captured him on the battlefield of Pavia. This was the cue for Henry's armies to march unopposed to Paris, the pay-off from ten years of investment in Wolsey's devious diplomacy. But, to the frustrated disappointment of both Henry and his Cardinal, Charles saw no reason to cut England in on a victory he had achieved almost entirely through his own efforts. He had not emptied his treasury to give Henry and his scheming Cardinal French land with which to make mischief.

Furious, Wolsey attempted to engineer a *volte-face* even more astonishing than the one with which he had burst upon Europe in 1514. If the Emperor would not support England, then England would not support him. The Cardinal had been secretly negotiating for some months with the Pope and a clique of other Italian rulers who were tired of Charles's domination of Italy. The moment Francis I was released by Charles at the beginning of 1526, he too was brought in on the anti-Imperial plot, but the equation was, in the end, unsound. The conspirators – England, France, the Pope and the Italians – were simply no match for the Emperor. In May 1527 Charles's troops ran riot in Rome and the Pope became effectively an Imperial prisoner. Early in 1529 the French were again shattered by Charles's armies, this time at Landriano, and Francis, without consulting England, made the best of a bad job and sued for peace at Cambrai. The Emperor Charles controlled

most of Europe, so France considered herself lucky to be left largely with her own frontiers. And England was, as she had been in the past, quietly ignored.

After fifteen years' scheming and ceaseless hard work, Cardinal Wolsey's European policy was exposed for the megalomaniac fantasy it had, essentially, always been. France and the Emperor had never truly needed to come cap-in-hand to England. When they had appeared to do so it had been simply to serve their own short-term and selfish ends. Henry had, of course, shared his Cardinal's delusions of English grandeur, particularly when they had seemed close to achievement. But now humiliated and out on a limb, the King's solution was simple. It was all Wolsey's fault, and the great Cardinal would have to pay the price. Besides, obsessed with all his European intriguings, Wolsey had let things go badly wrong at home.

England's foreign policy had been cripplingly expensive. In the years before Wolsey's rise to power, Henry had managed to squander most of the royal wealth accumulated in the previous reign. Between his accession and 12 June 1513, the Treasurer of

Siege warfare in the early sixteenth century, woodcut from Holinshed's *Chronicles*. The illustration shows the use of firearms to reduce the town, while knights in full armour await to attack.

the Chamber, the principal financial office, paid out over a million pounds, some two-thirds of which was spent on war and nearly a half of which was paid out in one week, 5–12 June 1513, preparing for the campaign against France. In the honeymoon years Parliament was called to raise extra money, pocket money almost, to be spent in addition to Henry's personal wealth. But by the 1520s Parliamentary subsidies had become a matter of survival, and as early as 1515 there had been trouble. In that year, when Wolsey wished to export English treasure to pay Continental allies and mercenaries, Parliament would only vote enough supplies to make up for the fact that previous grants had never been collected in full. An infuriated Wolsey urged Parliament's rapid dissolution and only one more was summoned in his fourteen years of supremacy. He did not like Parliament, trust Parliament or know how to handle it, and, the trouble that he had with the Parliament that met in 1523 showed Henry exactly what the Cardinal's failings were and what a handicap they could prove. For some four months the Commons stubbornly refused Wolsey's demands for money, and their resistance hardened when Wolsey himself turned up to make a hectoring and aggressive speech. The Cardinal had, only the previous year, collected by royal warrant a forced loan intended to yield £200,000. Now he asked, in addition, for a levy of four shillings in the pound. Parliament eventually agreed to half this, and not all at once; the subsidy must be spread over several years.

Wolsey's solution was simple. He coolly ignored the nation's representatives and the following year he sent out commissioners to make a compulsory levy on all men of property. He called the levy an Amicable Grant, but that did not disguise the fact that commissioners were still out collecting the compulsory loan of 1522, that a second set were enforcing immediate 'anticipated' payment of the 1523 subsidy, and that that subsidy was supposed, in any case, to repay the forced 'borrowings' of the previous year.

Resistance was widespread. In East Anglia and Kent there were even signs of armed rebellion. Henry intervened and snubbed Wolsey openly. He claimed no knowledge of the Amicable Grant and cancelled its compulsory demands immediately. He ordered the Council to enquire into the affair

64

and issued royal pardons to all who had resisted the Cardinal's
exactions. It was a sharp warning to Wolsey, too, of the speed
and lack of scruple with which Henry could divest himself of
cumbersome commitments.

The great Cardinal was now an object of general detestation.
Henry's repudiation of the Amicable Grant was taken to imply
that Wolsey was robbing the King to feather his own nest.
Wrote the poet Skelton, a client of Thomas Howard, formerly
Earl of Surrey, and who now as Duke of Norfolk led the group
of Court aristocrats dedicated to bringing down the great
Cardinal:

> And useth such abusion
> That in the conclusion
> All cometh to confusion.
> He is so ambitious
> So shameless, and so vicious,
> And so superstitious
> And so much oblivious
> From whence he came ...

Wolsey in fact, stole little from the royal coffers. Given the
extravagant character of his schemes, he spent Henry's money
as economically as anyone else could have managed. The true
source of his personal fortune – and the object of his peculation
– was the Church. And it was through the Church, to which he
owed so much and which he so indifferently rewarded, that his
destruction eventually came.

It had been the Church which had made it possible for Henry
to marry his brother's widow. Now Henry wanted the Church
to make it possible for him to set aside Catherine of Aragon,
and Wolsey, the Pope's special representative in England, should
be able to manage it if anyone could. It seemed a simple matter
to both the King and the Cardinal. But they were both wrong,
and it was the Cardinal who paid the price of failure.

By the 1520s Henry VIII had ceased to be a loving husband.
Catherine remained loyal and piously devoted, but, now
approaching forty – five year older than her husband – she was
wrinkled and somewhat dumpy. She was not the attractive
woman for whom Henry had jousted in the halcyon days that
opened the reign. Then he had worn her initials on his sleeve

and called himself 'Sir Loyal Heart'. When he returned from France in 1513, he had ridden hell-for-leather to Richmond to lay at her feet the keys of the two towns he had captured.

But it had been just after this occasion, during the New Year festivities of 1514, that the King's eye was caught by one of the Queen's ladies-in-waiting, Elizabeth Blount, the cousin of Lord Mountjoy. She was a pretty, forward girl, who returned Henry's interest with lively vigour. She became his mistress, bearing him, in 1519, a healthy son, and it was this little boy who proved to be one of the moving factors in the King's 'great matter', which brought down Wolsey and, thereafter, the Pope's authority in England.

For good wife though she was, Catherine of Aragon had failed in her primary function, to provide Henry with a healthy male heir. It had not been for lack of trying. She had borne her first baby on 31 January 1510, only seven months after her marriage. It had been a daughter, still-born. Within a year she produced a son, living and apparently healthy, but then the child had sickened and died. 1513 saw the birth of another boy, and 1514 yet another, but neither survived. In that same year, Queen Catherine, whose life had become a ceaseless, desperate round of pregnancies and childbeds, was delivered prematurely of a fourth son, still-born. Not until 18 February 1516 did she finally produce for her husband and his kingdom a sturdy, living child, and then it was a girl, christened after Henry's favourite sister, Mary. The King put a brave face on it. 'We are both young. If it was a daughter this time, by the grace of God the sons will follow.'

'By the grace of God' was an ominous phrase. Henry and Catherine had always been a pious couple. The Church possessed few children more devoted and scrupulous in their observance. Yet despite their religious enthusiasm, and despite their tireless conjugal efforts which, following the birth of Mary, resulted in several more pregnancies, after ten years of marriage England had no heir. Henry vowed solemnly to lead in person a crusade against the Turk if God would grant him a son. But no son came and, before long, even Catherine's abortive pregnancies ceased. Physicians summoned specially from Spain could not goad her exhausted system into quickening. It was tired of fertility, and who could blame it?

Miniature of Henry Fitzroy, Duke of Richmond, Henry's illegitimate son by Bessie Blount.

OPPOSITE Francis I King of France, a portrait by Jean Clouet.

69

It is doubtful whether Henry, in his deepest disappointment, ever blamed Catherine herself for her failure. She always inspired him with a certain respect. He was ever anxious to please her, perhaps even a little scared of her. And no one could deny that she had tried her hardest to give Henry a son. Had she been able to produce just one boy, the King would probably thereafter have discreetly enjoyed his mistresses and remained an affectionate husband, proud to appear in public with Catherine as his consort. In the turmoil of the divorce that was to come, one constant factor was Henry's wish to see Catherine reasonably cared for. Until she began actively and skilfully to thwart his plans he was not inspired by personal hatred or malice. He moved away from her more in sorrow than in anger.

His inspiration was, in fact, religious. Bessie Blount's son proved he could conceive a son. Catherine's non-stop pregnancies proved she was fertile. 'By the grace of God' he had been denied a male heir, and that was a catastrophe; the last time England had had a queen-regnant the country had been torn by civil war, and similar misfortunes had overtaken other countries.

And when Henry, pious theological scholar that he was, searched for an explanation of what he might have done to offend the Almighty, the answer was not far to seek. It lay in two texts right at the beginning of the Bible: 'Thou shalt not uncover the nakedness of thy brother's wife: it is thy brother's nakedness', (Leviticus, xviii, 16) and, again, from verse 21, chapter xx of the same book, 'If a man shall take his brother's wife, it is an unclean thing: he hath uncovered his brother's nakedness; they shall be childless.'

'If a man shall take his brother's wife, it is an unclean thing'

These texts did not directly refer to a *dead* brother, indeed their surface meaning was to prohibit adultery which deceived and betrayed the living. But the significance Henry attached to them was commonly accepted, and, indeed, had been accepted for some time. The two texts had been the very reason why, in 1503, both Henry VII and the Spanish ambassador had agreed to request from the Pope a special dispensation whereby Henry, Prince of Wales, might marry Catherine despite her previous relationship with Henry's elder brother, Arthur. And so it was that, some time before Catherine's fortieth birthday, in 1525, a 'great scruple' began to haunt Henry's mind. He later explained

70

that this came to him alone, as a result of 'assiduous study and erudition', and there is no reason to believe that the divorce project was not his own. He had no need of prompting about the words in Leviticus, and though Catherine's failure to produce a son was, as early as 1514, a subject of gossip and speculation, no one would have dared broach the subject directly with the King – not even Wolsey. Indeed, the Cardinal was so obsessed by the mesmerising treacheries of Europe's ever-changing political alliances, that he paid little heed to the nagging doubts that were advancing from the recesses of Henry's mind to consume, eventually, King, Cardinal, Court and country. When Henry first mentioned it to Wolsey, early in 1527, the Cardinal disliked the idea of an annulment or divorce and knelt down 'in his Privy Chamber ... the space of an hour or two, to persuade him from his will and appetite; but I could never bring to pass to dissuade him therefrom'.

In fact, Wolsey's initial attempt to persuade Henry 'from his will and appetite' is less likely to have been inspired by spiritual or moral than by political considerations. What worried the Cardinal was Catherine's relationship to the Emperor Charles and Charles's control over the Pope. But by 1527 Henry's mind was made up. He always was a man who experienced little difficulty in transforming his desires into the dictates of conscience, indeed, it was one of his strengths that he could reinforce his every conviction with rock solid moral authority and self-confidence. And once he discovered that he had, inadvertently, committed a sin – as he had, he believed, when he married Catherine of Aragon – then his determination to make amends became a chariot drawn by the galloping chargers of righteousness.

By 1527, furthermore, Henry was being spurred on by a lady every bit as wilful as himself and as cunning as Thomas Wolsey. The Catholic supporters of Queen Catherine were later to accuse Anne Boleyn of being a witch in league with the devil. They considered her malevolent intrigues to have been the prime cause of the catastrophe that brought down both Queen Catherine and the Roman Church in England – the new Church of England was the work of her cauldron and broomstick – and though this ludicrously exaggerates the personal influence of Anne Boleyn on English history, it scarcely

Thomas Wyatt the Elder, poet and courtier, who was one of the King's rivals for the favours of Anne Boleyn. Drawing by Holbein.

Tho: Wiatt Knight.

overstates her hold over the mind of Henry VIII. For several years he was infatuated by her, totally in thrall to her dark fascination: to reasons of State – the need for an heir – was added a third overwhelming factor – an irresistible torrent of passion.

Anne Boleyn's beauty was unconventional. 'Madame Anne', wrote a Venetian, 'is not one of the handsomest women in the world. She is of middling stature, swarthy complexion, long neck, wide mouth, bosom not much raised, and in fact has nothing but the King's great appetite – and her eyes, which are black and beautiful.' The eyes had it. When she fixed them on Henry he became, it seemed, her puppet.

She had no special advantages of birth. The Boleyns were wealthy merchants of London, one of whom had been Lord Mayor. Her mother was sister of Thomas Howard, the Duke of Norfolk, but Anne owed her rise in favour at Court to her own sister Mary, rather than to her parents, for after Bessie Blount had been packed off to the country with one of Wolsey's young protégés, Gilbert Tallboys, it was Mary Boleyn who became Henry's new mistress. When Anne came back from a period as lady-in-waiting to the Queen of France, she found her sister enjoying royal favour to the full. Anne became lady-in-waiting to Queen Catherine, and Sir Thomas Wyatt, the poet, made a play for her. Then Henry Percy, son of the Earl of Northumberland, made more honourable proposals, until Wolsey intervened personally to put an end to the romance. Anne never forgave the Cardinal for his interference, though Wolsey had probably acted at the behest of Henry who had, perhaps, already developed a personal interest in his mistress's dark young sister.

Whenever it was that Henry first openly declared his feelings for her, Anne Boleyn responded in a most unconventional fashion. She had no wish to follow the path of Elizabeth Blount or her sister, from obscurity to favour and back to obscurity again. If the King wanted her, he must make an honest woman of her. She retired from Court to her father's house at Hever in Kent.

Henry was not a writing man, but suddenly royal messengers began galloping down to Kent, bearing love letters penned painfully by the King's own hand. There could be no more sincere token of the royal affection than the fact that Henry was prepared to sit down and give himself a headache scratching out in Court French lumbering gallantries to this cunning teenage slip of a girl. 'If you would be a true loyal mistress and friend and give yourself body and heart to me, who have been and will be your most loyal servant (if your hardness does not forbid it), I promise you not only that the name will be yours by right, but also that I shall take you alone for my mistress, cast all others out of my thoughts and affections, and serve you only.' To such unambiguous promises, Anne sent back teasing

Mary Boleyn, Anne's elder sister. Mary became Henry's mistress in about 1520, and Anne owed much of her swift rise in favour at Court to her sister. Portrait after the style of Holbein.

replies. Henry worked himself into a frenzy of confused humility. 'I have endured great agony debating with myself the content of your letters, not knowing how to interpret them, whether to my disadvantage as demonstrated in one place, or to my advantage as in another. I implore you to let me know plainly your feelings concerning the love that is between us.'

Until he fell for Anne, Henry had toyed with a compromise solution to his dynastic dilemma. In 1525 Bessie Blount's son, who had been christened Henry Fitzroy and was now a blond and bulky six-year-old replica of his father, was created Duke of Richmond and Somerset – two significant titles. Henry VII had been Earl of Richmond before he ousted Richard III, and Duke of Somerset had been the title of his grandfather. The implication was obvious. If Henry could not be succeeded by a legitimate son, then the throne would go to his love-child. There was even talk of making the little Duke King of Ireland and marrying him to a foreign princess – English ambassadors being sent to Europe to explain that the boy 'is near of the King's blood and of excellent qualities, and is already furnished to the state of a great prince, and yet may be easily, by the King's means, exalted to higher things'. In all of this Queen Catherine acquiesced, in public at least. It looked as though judicious juggling and a little hypocrisy might solve the dynastic problem. The Pope was even prepared to grant a special dispensation so that Henry Fitzroy might marry his half-sister Mary, Henry's daughter by Catherine.

But Anne wanted a divorce and Henry wanted, if at all possible, a legitimate heir. So in May 1527 Wolsey set up a special tribunal in his London home before which Henry appeared to answer a charge of having, for eighteen years, unlawfully lived with the wife of his dead brother Arthur. It was an extraordinary and totally secret performance. Catherine and the Court knew nothing of it. Nor did the Pope. Wolsey was using his powers as the legatine representative of Rome in England. He was presumably hoping to hustle through an annulment and then secretly to negotiate the Pope's agreement.

It was a shady, dubious manœuvre, and events frustrated whatever chance of success it might have had, for on 1 June 1527 news reached London of the sack of Rome. The Pope was virtually a prisoner of the Emperor Charles, Catherine's

RIGHT Hever Castle, the Kent home of the Boleyn family. Anne's grandfather had converted the medieval fortress into a fine residence for his family.

BELOW Letter to Anne Boleyn, written in September 1528 in Henry's own handwriting.

74

nephew, who would never connive in such an underhand rejection of his aunt. Wolsey saw the point immediately. He shut down his tribunal and started angling for an alternative solution. The imprisoned Pope, Clement VII, would be persuaded to delegate his powers to Wolsey until such time as Charles released him from captivity, then Wolsey could annul Henry's old marriage, get the King remarried and present Pope Clement, whenever he was released, with a *fait accompli*.

But, though the whole plot depended on secrecy, Wolsey omitted to make this clear to his fellow conspirator who, on 22 June 1527, confronted his wife with the news that they had been living in sin for the past eighteen years. There had, of course, been rumours of an annulment circulating in London for months, but now Henry brazenly announced his intentions

75

Pope Clement VII, who found himself caught between Henry and Charles V in the great matter of Henry's divorce.

to the one person most likely to send the story straight to the Emperor Charles. And Catherine did precisely that. A servant from her household, one Felipez, came to Henry begging permission to visit his sick mother in Spain and claiming that Catherine had refused to let him go. Playing a game of double bluff for which he was totally unsuited, Henry 'knowing great collusion and dissimulation, did also dissimulate'. He let Felipez go, intending to have him waylaid in France to be produced later as evidence of Catherine's duplicity. But Henry was being too clever by half. Felipez outwitted his ambushers, got to Spain and spilled out the whole story to Charles, who promptly wrote to Catherine offering full support, to Henry requesting him to halt, and to the Pope asking him to take the whole matter in hand and to revoke Wolsey's authority. The cat was out of the bag. Henry's private scruple had become an issue of European power politics.

The King was fast losing confidence in 'his Cardinal'. Anne Boleyn took every opportunity of turning Henry against Wolsey, and her father, Sir Thomas Boleyn, Viscount Rochford and soon to be Earl of Wiltshire, was one of several powerful courtiers working for an end to Wolsey's dominance. In retaliation, and sadly misjudging his master's passions, Wolsey refused to take the royal affair with Anne seriously. If Henry got his annulment Wolsey would then marry him off to Renée, the sister-in-law of Francis I. Travelling grandly through France in the summer of 1527, trying simultaneously to organise an attack on Charles and to gain support for his improbable vice-regency for the imprisoned Pope, Wolsey grew dangerously out of touch with developments at home. Henry started to take initiatives without deigning to inform him. Wolsey was deliberately kept in the dark about a secret approach Henry made to Rome to gain not only an annulment of his marriage with Catherine but special facilities to marry Anne. The King was starting to act as the true master in his own house. He was flexing his political muscles and rather enjoying the sensation. When Wolsey got back from France in the summer of 1527 he discovered that Henry would no longer sign letters unseen and would only agree to receive him at such times as Anne Boleyn gave her approval. The writing for the great Cardinal was clearly on the wall.

76

ANNA BOLINA·VXOR— HENRI·OCTA

Anne Boleyn, Henry's second Queen, by an unknown artist.

Jane Seymour, Henry's third Queen: portrait by Holbein.

77

4
The
King's
New
Men
1528-9

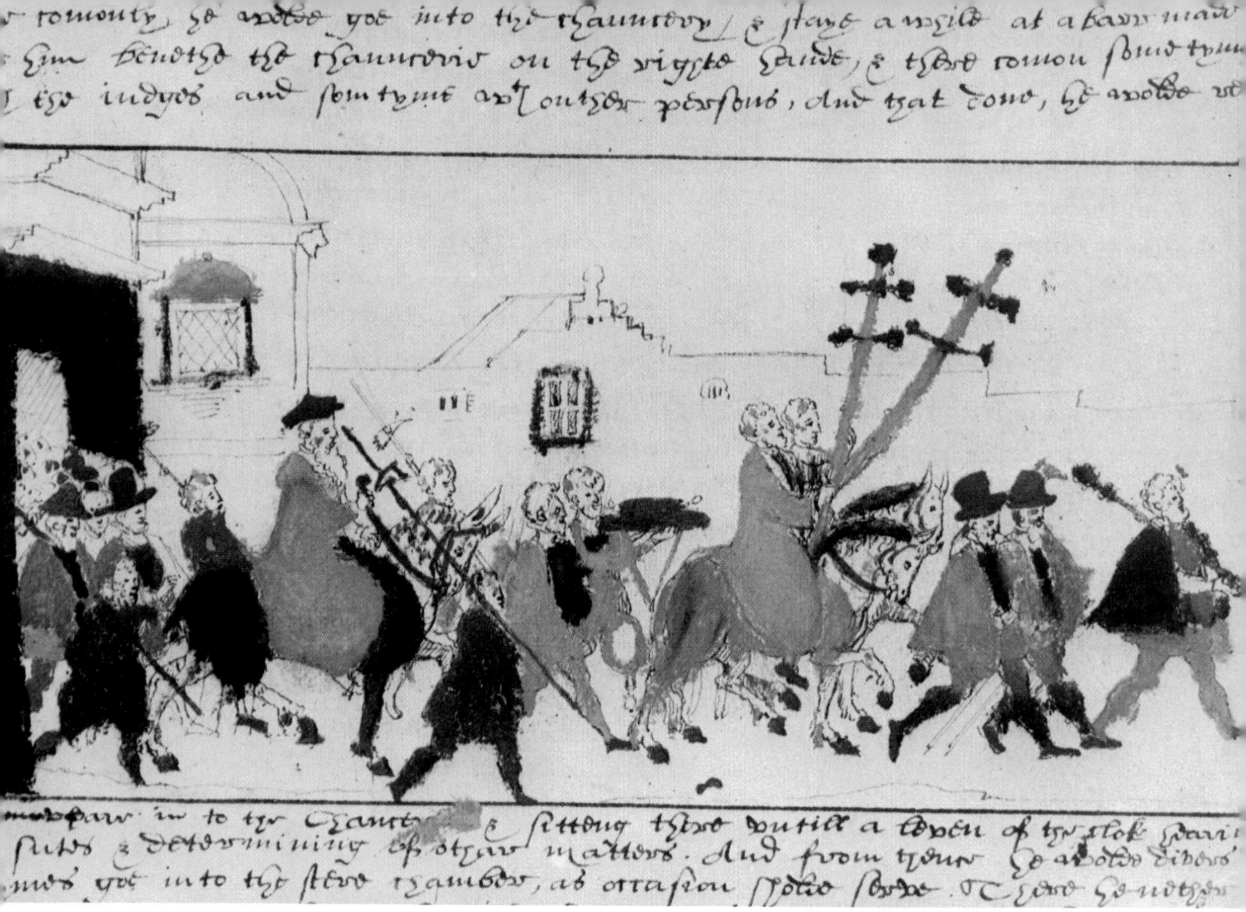

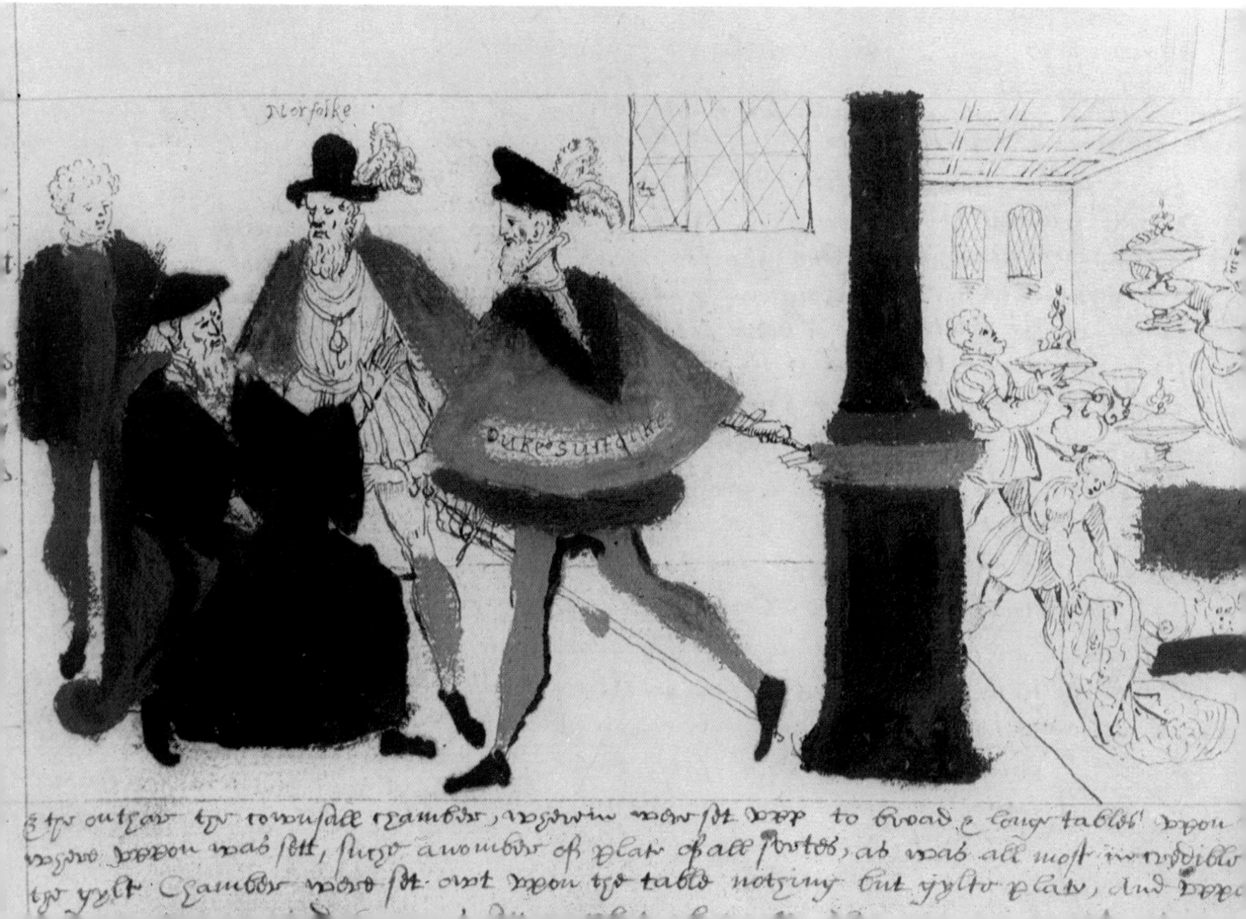
Norfolke
Duke Suffolke

THE SUMMER OF 1528 was hot and plague-ridden, people died in their thousands. It brought more business to the priests than the doctors, said the French ambassador. No one knew how to cope with the sweating sickness, and this particular epidemic was especially virulent. Men felt a slight pain in the head or heart, sweated, shivered and then died within three or four hours. This threw Henry into a panic, for the plague always terrified him. To avoid it he usually spent the summer months out of London. This year he departed even more rapidly, keeping constantly on the move, dosing himself with a succession of noxious potions, confessing daily and hearing at least three Masses every twenty-four hours. He dictated several wills. His fear was the more graceless in that he was fleeing from Anne Boleyn, who had been taken ill when the epidemic struck the Court. He wrote consolingly to her that the sweat seemed more lenient when it lodged in female victims, and he larded his epistles liberally with his heavy expressions of affection. But he requested her firmly not to come back to him too soon. One could not be too careful.

Wolsey's entourage started falling with the plague. The Cardinal promptly halted the legal term and left London for Hampton Court. The only lawyers with work to do were the notaries, who turned out wills by the score. Henry was anxious to learn what remedy the Cardinal was using to keep the sweat at bay. He advised Wolsey to eat and drink moderately and to take 'Rasis' pills once a week; the Cardinal should follow Henry's example and put his spiritual life in order.

In matters of survival Henry's agility and industry could be tireless. The previous winter, disillusioned with Wolsey's failure to get quick results, he had taken matters into his own hands and sent several embassies to the Pope. Had they succeeded, the prospect for Wolsey would have been gloomy. But they had achieved no more than the Cardinal, indeed Wolsey was able to point out with some glee the elementary mistakes in the documents they brought back, while Wolsey's own representatives, Stephen Gardiner, his secretary, and Edward Fox, the King's almoner, extracted from Pope Clement an agreement to let the whole matter be heard in England. So through this long, hot, plague-ridden summer, the Cardinal, for the moment back in favour, eagerly awaited with Henry the arrival of

81

not disobaye his louing request, what socver in his harte ys founde towards ty Cardinall but toke incontinent his tablet of golde & gaue at his goode

The King sends his physician to treat Wolsey, who lies in his bed, shown at the top right-hand corner. (Bodleian Ms. Douce 363, folio 76). BELOW Instrument case of Henry's barber surgeon, with the royal arms and Tudor Rose decorated upon its top.

Clement's special representative, Cardinal Lorenzo Campeggio, who had in the past served England's interests in Rome so well that Henry had given him the title and revenues of the bishopric of Salisbury. Campeggio should cause little trouble. Once this sweating sickness was over, Henry could look forward to some comparatively anxiety-free days.

But matters were not as straightforward as they appeared on the surface. Campeggio was a gouty old man, who could not travel fast. But even for an invalid, the time he took to reach England from Rome was inordinately long – four months instead of six weeks. Though Clement had first granted Campeggio's commission in April, the old Cardinal Legate did not reach London until 9 October. And his infuriating procrastination, which he stolidly maintained after he attained his journey's end, was by politic design. Clement, who did not

dare to offend the Emperor Charles, was playing for time and had given Campeggio strict instructions to do the same. And this was precisely what Campeggio did. Before getting involved in the rights and wrongs of the annulment, he insisted with firm naïveté on the pastoral responsibilities of his clerical calling, and sought to heal the breach between Henry and Catherine and to rekindle love that had long since flickered out. Henry was flabbergasted and – as Campeggio had hoped – flatly refused to co-operate, threatening that if things went wrong England would desert Rome for the heretical Lutheranism of the German princes.

Next Henry turned up at his visitor's lodgings, and hectored Campeggio so loudly that every word could be heard in the

Thomas Boleyn, Earl of Wiltshire and of Ormonde, father of Anne and Mary Boleyn. Drawing by Holbein.

The seal of Cardinal Lorenzo Campeggio, who arrived in England in September 1528 to preside over the ecclesiastical court at Blackfriars, which was to hear the matrimonial dispute between Henry and Catherine of Aragon.

next room. So Campeggio tried his second ploy: to inveigle Catherine into a nunnery – and this met with a somewhat more enthusiastic response from the offended spouse than had the first initiative. Indeed, for a day or so, the King was thoroughly taken by the notion. It was convenient, cheap and totally respectable. The most scandalous rumours were causing disturbances in London. Though Campeggio's mission was theoretically a secret, as indeed was Henry's whole project of remarriage, it took little guessing to work out what was afoot. Poor old Campeggio was most alarmed, as he was helped into his barge, to be jostled by crowds shouting 'No Nan Bullen for us!' Catherine was a popular Queen, while Anne, tarred with the brush of her sister's reputation, and herself no crowd-pleaser, was generally detested. But Catherine soon scotched that suggestion. First, Campeggio and Wolsey went to see her, then Henry tried blustering, Campeggio saw her alone, then the two Cardinals again tried a joint attack – Wolsey even falling on his knees – and finally a deputation of bishops attempted a mass onslaught – all to no avail. Catherine, growing daily in dignity, piety and unshakable conviction, would not be moved. Her only concession was the suggestion that she would become a nun if Henry became, and remained, a monk. Quite apart from her pride and her material interests in the contro-versy, Catherine had come to believe that Henry was embarking upon a course which not only imperilled his own soul, but would destroy hers as well if she allowed him to declare her daughter a bastard and herself a harlot.

Public opinion was to both Henry and Wolsey a matter of crowds cheering their processions through the streets; its motives and discontents did not concern them. But now, while Campeggio from his sick bed talked of not opening his court until Christmas or even the New Year, Henry woke up to the unpopularity of his attempts to get rid of Catherine. His 'Great Matter' was splitting the nation and even men of good will found it difficult to support the King. The Queen was described by one courtier as 'beloved as if she had been of the blood royal of England'.

Henry decided that some exercise in public relations was called for, so on 8 November 1528 he summoned to his presence a collection of nobles, judges, aldermen and other notables to

84

explain to them 'the sores that trouble my mind ... the pangs that trouble my conscience'. He invited them to share his perplexity.

> As you well know [he said] Catherine is a woman of most gentleness, of most humility and buxomness, yea, and of all good qualities appertaining to nobility. She is without comparison, as I this twenty years almost have had true experiment, so that if I were to marry again – if the marriage might be good – I would surely choose her above all other women.

The trouble was that 'although it hath pleased Almighty God to send us a fair daughter of a noble woman and me, begotten to our great comfort and joy, yet it hath been told us by diverse great clerks, that neither she is our lawful daughter nor her mother our lawful wife'. Should Cardinal Campeggio now find that these diverse great clerks were wrong, then Henry would, of course, be delighted again to embrace Catherine as his true and lawful wife. Indeed 'there was never thing more pleasant nor acceptable to me in my life'.

The naked dishonesty of the royal confusion impressed no one. Henry still appeared in public with Catherine as his consort, but the disrepair their marriage had fallen into was common knowledge. 'Some sighed and said nothing', and after Henry's over-naïve address, 'every man spoke as his heart served him.' Catherine's sympathisers were more numerous than Henry had bargained for and now, in the winter of 1528, Catherine herself suddenly struck back at her husband with an astonishing blow that demolished the painstaking work of over two years. The royal case was based upon the flaws alleged to lie in the original dispensation by which the Pope had authorised the marriage of Henry to his brother's widow. Now Catherine produced another papal brief, issued at the same time and sent to Spain, which was worded in such a way that the very objections which Henry was now making were all answered. Spanish envoys had, apparently, brought a copy of this alternative document to Catherine in the spring, and she had held onto it quietly for six months before dramatically releasing it to Campeggio.

Henry and Wolsey were thunderstruck. Their first reaction was to denounce this alternative dispensation as a forgery – and its sudden appearance from nowhere was indeed convenient.

But, if it were a forgery, they would still have to prove their contention not from a copy but from the original brief, and Catherine's nephew Charles had the original document safely under lock and key in Spain. He showed it to English ambassadors and let them peruse it carefully, but he was not so foolish as to let the document permanently into the hands of such interested parties. Henry was enraged. After Campeggio's infuriating shilly-shallying this was too much. He struck back at Catherine viciously. The Privy Council declared her a menace to the safety of the King: she was inciting popular violence that might endanger the King's life; she could no longer share the royal bed or board, nor see her daughter, the Princess Mary; she was sent away from Hampton Court to Greenwich and, as a crowning injury, Anne Boleyn was moved into her apartments. Henry would no longer maintain his public pretence at marital harmony. In the hope of being granted leave at least to see her daughter, Catherine weakened to the extent of writing for Henry's benefit to her nephew to request him to let the English have the document they wanted – but she sent it by a messenger who explained to Charles exactly what was going on and that he must hang on to the brief at all costs.

To Campeggio, Catherine's *coup* descended miraculously. It was a manna from heaven – the very excuse he needed to postpone the hearing he was coming to dread. Not until 18 June 1529, fifteen months after the Pope had initially commissioned it and eight months after Campeggio had arrived in London, did the extraordinary tribunal finally open at Blackfriars. And then Catherine again delighted the papal party, for she came in person to appeal that the case be heard in Rome by His Holiness himself. When Henry appeared later to rehearse, yet again, his scruples, Catherine ignored all formality, rushed from her seat and knelt at his feet begging him not to dishonour her and her daughter. 'Sir' she sobbed, her English becoming more and more broken as her emotions overcame her, 'I beseech you for all the love that hath been between us, and for the love of God, let me have justice and right. Take of me some pity and compassion, for I am a poor woman and a stranger born out of your dominion. I have no assured friend here.' Embarrassed and silent, Henry sat motionless, as though there were no woman weeping at his feet. 'When ye had me at the first', cried

86

Catherine, 'I take God to be my judge, I was a true maid, without touch of man. And whether this be true or no, I put it to your conscience.' The tension in the court room became unbearable, but still Henry said nothing. 'If there be any just cause by the law that you can allege against me', went on Catherine, her white, strained features framed by her plain black dress, 'I am well content to depart to my great shame and dishonour.' But this court could not decide that and therefore she would have none of it. She rose to her feet and swept out.

Three times the usher called 'Catherina, Queen of England, come into the court', but his cries went unheeded. Catherine would never return. And Campeggio knew then that his ordeal was at an end. For now that the Queen had appealed so formally and openly to Rome, the Pope could not possibly allow the matter finally to be settled in London. Henry remained speechless.

The court dragged on. John Fisher, the Bishop of Rochester, conducted a most virulent and brilliant defence for Catherine in her absence, but it was not necessary. At the end of July 1529 Campeggio rose to announce that since all the papal courts went into adjournment during the long Roman summer, and since this tribunal was a papal court, the case would be held over for three months until October. Henry's rage was towering and he sent the Dukes of Norfolk and Suffolk to insist that the court continue in session until it reached a decision. But Campeggio was adamant. 'By the Mass', shouted Suffolk in open court, striking 'a great clap on the table', 'now I see that the old said saw is true, that there was never legate or cardinal that did good in England.'

If the adjournment was a defeat for Henry, it was a disaster for Wolsey. For it was not long before papal messengers arrived summoning the whole proceeding, and Henry himself, to Rome. The threat in Suffolk's courtroom protest became a grim reality. Wolsey had tried and had failed. The King had been ordered to go humbly to Rome and kneel at the feet of the Pope. He had been humiliated before the eyes of London, England and the whole of Europe. From the moment the divorce had first been mooted, the Cardinal had been in peril, for even if he had succeeded, he would simply have been yielding sway to Anne Boleyn, her father and the nobles like

'When ye had me at the first ... I was a true maid, without touch of man'

Norfolk and Suffolk who had joined with the Boleyns against him. Now that he had failed, he would have to pay the price.

By the time Campeggio formally took his leave of England, men were talking openly of the great Cardinal's imminent disgrace. Indeed, Wolsey had to ask Campeggio to beg special permission for him to attend the Legate's farewell audience on 19 September 1529. When the two churchmen rode into Court Campeggio was conducted to special lodgings, but Wolsey was told that his usual apartments were occupied. He had to borrow a friend's room to change out of his riding clothes. He walked into the Presence Chamber expecting the worst and fell at the King's feet. To his astonishment – and that of the Court – Henry smiled, raised him up, and led him off to the window for a long discussion. Then the King dined with Anne – a bad sign – but after dinner sought out Wolsey again and talked earnestly and closely with him for some time. They would discuss more next day, it was agreed, and Wolsey, still without lodgings, rode off into the night in search of a bed.

The next morning, however, when the Cardinal got back to Court, he found Henry in the saddle ready not for discussing affairs of State but for a day's riding arranged by Anne Boleyn – who had also, by her special labour, carefully laid on a lunch which meant that the King would not be back until night-fall. By that time Wolsey was due to be far away escorting Campeggio on the first stage of his journey towards Rome. The Cardinal who believed himself a match for any man in

Drawing of Wolsey's funeral at Leicester Abbey, from Cavendish's life of Wolsey. The Cardinal died at Leicester on 29 November 1530, on his way from York to London, where he was to stand trial.
(Bodleian Ms. Douce 363, folio 91).

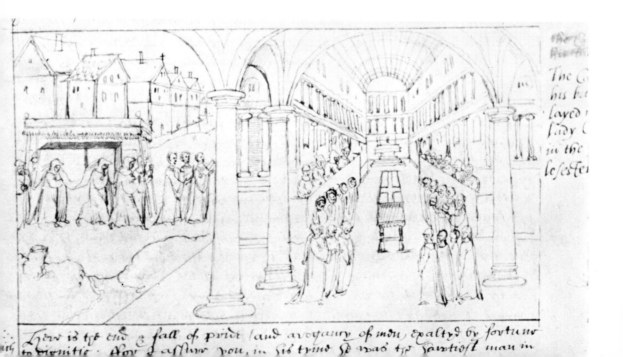

Thomas Howard, third Duke of Norfolk; portrait by Holbein. He is shown holding the white staff of the Lord Treasurership.

Europe had been out-manœuvred by a woman. Two days later Suffolk and Norfolk delightedly ordered him to surrender the Lord Chancellor's great seal. Wolsey proudly refused, demanding to see the King's written authority, but when he saw Henry's handwriting on the writ he broke down and cried.

On 29 November 1530, after fourteen agonising months stripped of power, wealth and finally of hope and health, Cardinal Thomas Wolsey breathed his last at Leicester, travelling under arrest to face trial, sentence and, certainly, the block. 'If' he exclaimed on his deathbed, 'I had served God as diligently as I have done my King, He would not have given me over in my grey hairs.' Only his arrogance stayed with him to the end, and even that was tempered with a certain remorse.

'A Royal Martyrdom'

Henry was a great huntsman and spent many hours in the saddle, even in his later years, when he became extremely heavy and gross. One courtier described the King as sparing 'no pains to convert the sport of hunting into a royal martyrdom'. Anne Boleyn enthusiastically joined Henry in his hunting and hawking, for Catherine of Aragon had loved the sport and grew especially jealous when she was excluded. It was considered by some that Henry had political motives in these hunting progresses, for it would accustom people in country districts to the idea that Anne might well become Queen.

Robert Cheseman, the King's falconer; portrait by Holbein.

Hunting party for the Emperor Charles v at the Castle of Torgan; painting by Lucas Cranach the Elder.

'Let us cease to
sing the praises of
the English Nero'

If Henry VIII had died at the same time as his great Cardinal, his reign would scarcely have been a memorable one. By November 1530 he had ruled for over twenty-one years. Approaching his fortieth birthday, Henry had lived gloriously, extravagantly and to little effect. He had squandered his father's fortune, won some passing victories in France, and let England become the instrument of Wolsey's personal and vain ambition. He had developed no mechanism for ruling the country more efficiently or for securing his authority more effectively. Hunting, hawking, banqueting, dancing and music-making, he had ruled like a Nero. Fortunately England had not burnt.

And by 1530 Henry was not the handsome young man that he had been twenty years previously. Already he was afflicted with the corpulence that was in old age to immobilise him, a vast rotting hulk transported by servants, litters, ropes and pulleys. In his thirties and forties he still spent hours in the saddle, hunting or jousting, but two nasty accidents had somewhat reduced his passion for that particular form of entertainment. In March 1524 he had been playing at Hector and Achilles in the lists with his brother-in-law Suffolk, when he forgot to lower his visor. The crowd saw the danger, but Henry thought their warning shouts were encouragements to ride faster, so he thundered delightedly along the barrier gathering speed, until Suffolk's lance struck and shattered into a thousand piercing splinters which shot into the King's headpiece. Henry could have been killed or blinded, but he escaped. And to prove the sort of man he was, he rode a further six courses, though presumably he was most shockingly bruised.

A year later he was hawking on foot near Hitchin. Confronted with a wide ditch he ran at it with a pole, intending to vault across. Unfortunately, the pole could not bear his vast weight, snapped, and catapulted the King head first into the mud. It would have been a highly comical scene, had not Henry's head been stuck so fast that he could not remove it and began to choke. If a footman had not hauled the royal body swiftly from the morass, Henry 'had been drowned'. But purple-faced and spluttering the King survived and, we can presume, probably hawked half an hour more to prove that the upset had not hurt him. He was a man of stubborn pride.

But, as Henry was getting more and more involved in the

infuriating complications and delays that hedged about his first attempt to remarry, he was struck down by a more sinister complaint. Early in 1514 he had been laid low with a bout of smallpox and in 1521 had been bitten by a mosquito which gave him malaria. He shrugged off both illnesses, though it was from them, perhaps, that he developed his hysterical fear of the plague and sweating sickness. Now, probably in 1528, an ulcer appeared on one of his legs that was to stay with him till he died. It was to spread to both legs and, eventually, to immobilise him completely. Historians have usually assumed that the ulcers were syphilitic and that Henry passed on the hereditary symptoms of this terrible disease to his children. But his latest biographer, Dr Scarisbrick, has found no evidence for this assumption. There was an established sixteenth-century mercury treatment for syphilis, which is never mentioned in the medical documents relating to Henry's life – though that might have been, of course, a consequence of discretion. Dr Scarisbrick believes that Henry's ever more agonising ulcers were varicose, a consequence of varicose veins. His constant exercise and the savagely ignorant medical treatment of the day 'would have caused the veins to become thrombosed, the leg to swell and an extremely painful chronic ulcer to develop on his thigh'.

Sir Arthur McNalty, the learned author of *Henry VIII, a Difficult Patient* (1952) has suggested that Henry may have suffered from osteomyelitis. This is a chronic, septic infection which could have attacked Henry's thighbone after a jousting injury. The symptoms are as unpleasant as those of a varicose ulcer. Pus is discharged and, from time to time, splinters of necrosed bone work their way agonisingly to the surface. But the pain of this particular affliction is intermittent. The sufferer can enjoy periods of remission when the condition dies down – and it would seem that Henry's legs were not a constant torture. So perhaps osteomyelitis is the most convincing diagnosis to be made from the distant and patchy evidence available. At all events, from the end of the 1520s onwards, after the fall of Wolsey, Henry VIII was certainly afflicted quite regularly with fierce and terrible pains in the legs which, along with the headaches that he had always suffered from, made him an increasingly peppery, irascible and unpredictable King of England.

The most difficult thing to predict in 1530 was what would become of the King's 'Great Matter'. The men who had worked so hard to oust Wolsey and to hound him after his fall were small men, unable to supply from their own ranks a successor as Lord Chancellor. The lynch-pin of the cabal, Thomas Boleyn, Viscount Rochford, had reached his eminence simply because of his daughter's sudden importance. Charles Brandon, Duke of Suffolk, also owed his position to unusual royal favour, while his romantic marriage to Mary, the King's sister, brought him too close to the throne for Henry to trust him with any more power. Thomas Howard, Duke of Norfolk, uncle of Anne Boleyn and Wolsey's greatest enemy, was also already too powerful to be trusted further. There remained Stephen Gardiner, a loyal and hard-working servant of the King, but he was also a cleric, and Henry would never again make a church-man Chancellor. For that position he selected Sir Thomas More, a trained lawyer who was conscientious, eminent and respected. Henry had known More for many years, enjoyed his company and felt for him affection, if not love. More was, of course, an international figure, celebrated with Erasmus and Colet for his humanism and his elegant taste for the New Learning. 'A man of angel's wit,' pronounced the grammarian Robert Whittington, 'I know not his fellow. For where is the man of that gentleness, lowliness and affability? And, as time requireth, a man of marvellous mirth and pastimes, and sometimes of as sad gravity. A man for all seasons.' An apt title, though More, in the last resort, did not adapt precisely as his master required. He was also, unfortunately for Henry, a most devout son of the Church who had the very deepest feelings about the King's proposed divorce. He believed, quite simply, that Henry and Catherine were rightfully joined together in holy matrimony and could never be put asunder. And to that belief he held firm. When Henry first asked him to become his Chancellor, More, who could see what trouble lay ahead, refused. But Henry would not take no for an answer. He angrily insisted that More accept the honour he was being offered. And the King conceded that he would never compel his new Chancellor to act in matters that offended his beliefs. The divorce, he promised, would be prosecuted only by men 'whose consciences could well enough agree therein'. More could 'look first unto

VTOPIAE INSVLAE FIGVRA

Map of Utopia, from the first edition of Sir Thomas More's *Utopia*, printed in Louvain in 1516. This copy belonged to Cuthbert Tunstall, Bishop of Durham.

God, and after God unto him'. Which is precisely what More did, so that, though Henry had got himself an excellent and thorough Chancellor, he had no one to take Wolsey's place in the great business which lay closest of all to the King's heart and which had become, indeed, the consuming centre and goal of his entire policy.

Henry would have to look after himself – and this he did, remarkably and, despite previous evidence to the contrary, with surprising skill and purpose. Looking at his twenty years of semi-indolence, and the eight years in the 1530s when he was to leave much day-to-day strategy in the hands of Thomas

The title page of Henry VIII's *Assertio Septem Sacramentorum*, in which he attacked the ideas of Martin Luther.

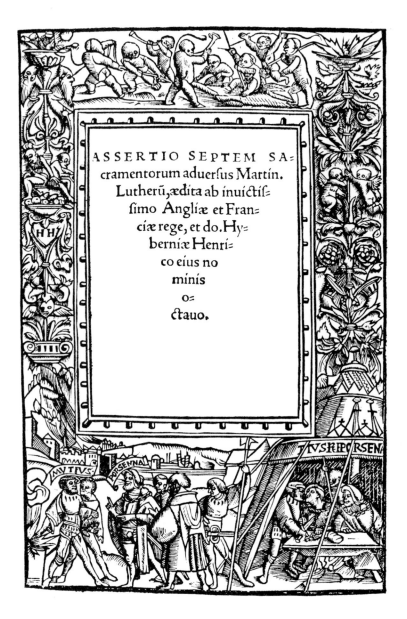

ASSERTIO SEPTEM SA=
cramentorum aduerſus Martin.
Lutherũ,ædita ab inuictiſ=
ſimo Angliæ et Fran=
ciæ rege, et do.Hy=
berniæ Henri=
co eius no
minis
o=
ctauo.

Cromwell, historians have found it difficult to believe that Henry himself decisively swung national policy in the direction of actually denying the Pope's authority in England and severing the English Church from Rome. Yet in the years after the fall of Wolsey there is no evidence to suggest that any of Henry's new advisers were firmly pushing him in any particular direction, and every reason indeed, to believe that Henry made his own decisions.

96

Henry was a good Catholic, and remained so until he died. Through all his arguments with the Pope and his eventual rejection of Roman authority Henry remained a religious conservative. The token of this that is most striking to modern eyes is the royal title which is inscribed on all British coins to this day 'F.D.', *Fidei Defensor* – Defender of the Faith – a title given to Henry by the Pope, and proudly preserved by Henry through all his quarrels with the Pontiff.

The way in which Henry earned the papal accolade was significant. In the summer of 1521 there appeared in London a lengthy treatise entitled *Assertio Septem Sacramentorum – The Defence of the Seven Sacraments* – which, with more ardour than elegance, set out the Catholic arguments against the new heresy that Martin Luther was propagating in Germany. It was aimed particularly at Luther's book of 1520, *De Captivitate Babylonica – The Babylonian Captivity* – and was introduced to the world in a grand ceremony at the great cross outside St Paul's Cathedral, where sermons were preached to mass audiences each Sunday, on 12 May 1521. Some books of Luther's were solemnly burned – and Wolsey wielded in his hand – like some sword of Damocles – *The Defence of the Seven Sacraments*, which turned out to be written by no less an author than the King himself. A few days later Henry wrote to the Pope to announce his intention of dedicating the work to him and, when the book was printed, some thirty copies were despatched, in August, to Rome, one of them specially adorned with verses selected by Wolsey and copied out by Henry himself. This one was for the Pope. The others were for the cardinals.

The very improbability of the King of England forswearing the saddle for months to pore long hours over theological terms and, finally, to compose such a volume was the very reason Henry did it – and by all accounts he really did compose the work himself. *The Defence of the Seven Sacraments* became a best-seller, not just in England – that was only to be expected – but all over Europe. It went through twenty editions in the sixteenth century, being published in many cities including Antwerp, Rome, Frankfurt, Cologne and Paris. It became the focus of a formidable little corpus of polemical work, scholars leaping to its attack or defence. It was all very gratifying for a King known previously only for his physical accomplishments.

The Golden Bull of Clement VII; which confirmed Leo X's granting of the title of Defender of the Faith to Henry VIII.

Henry was delighted to display a dimension beyond all his fellow kings – especially in 1520. The Field of the Cloth of Gold was his worldly triumph, the book his spiritual success.

The Pope's reaction was even more enthusiastic than Henry and Wolsey could have hoped, for the moment the English embassy put the book in his hands the Pontiff began to read it keenly, nodding his head and muttering little comments of appreciation as he went along. He indignantly refused a suggestion that Henry's dedicatory verses might be read out to him, but insisted on deciphering the royal handwriting himself. Indeed, he was so pleased with the verses that he read them three times. He praised the whole volume '*super sidera*' – to the skies.

Wolsey and Henry had been trying for years to secure the sort of title which the Most Christian King of France and His Catholic Majesty of Spain enjoyed, and now, on 11 October 1521, the Pope bestowed upon the King of England the honour 'Defender of the Faith'. The grant was intended for Henry alone, and not for his heirs, but despite the fact that in years to come Henry was to reject the faith he had so valiantly defended in 1521, and despite the fact that most of his successors have stood by his rejection, his painfully-won title has stuck. 'King of Ireland' and 'Emperor of India' have passed away – but 'F.D.' lives on.

It is not quite so inconsistent as it sounds. Henry's book was written to defend the true faith against Martin Luther in particular, and though his divorce campaign eventually gathered such momentum that he found himself denying the authority of the Pope, Henry's Reformation never embraced the Lutheran creed. The break with Rome was precisely described by its title: the denial of the power of the Bishop of Rome, but not the denial of hierarchical religious power and might *per se*. Henry appropriated as much of that as he could for himself and the English monarchy. The wealth of the Church was also plundered, but again so that its new master, Henry, could use it as he, the new Head of the Church, saw fit. The faith itself remained intact, with Henry giving himself even more power and wealth to defend it.

The first steps towards the breach had, in 1530, already been taken. Campeggio's announcement that the whole divorce would have to be considered in Rome had been a predictable, but decisive turning point. For it simply was not in Henry's nature to accept that he or his servants should travel to Rome meekly to accept the Pope's verdict, even if it turned out to be favourable to him. The King of England would have to become a suitor – a beggar for the favours of an institution which, in Henry's own realm, was *his* servant. By pulling the divorce case out of England – and emphasising his own, Rome-based authority, Clement had in fact made the Church in England the next battlefield of the long-drawn-out campaign. Henry would fight where he was strongest, on his own home ground.

For though Henry had comparatively slender domestic support for his attempts to exchange Catherine of Aragon for Anne Boleyn, there was a strong body of English feeling which endorsed his new tactic – to attack the power and privileges of the Roman Church in England. Wolsey's conspicuous pomp and arrogance had symbolised what was wrong in an institution for which many people had lost their respect. The Church was wealthy – incredibly wealthy. It probably owned over a third of all the land in England, more than the King and certainly more than any single noble. And even individual ecclesiastics, like the abbots of Glastonbury and St Albans, or the bishops of

Winchester and Durham, enjoyed incomes greater than those of any temporal lord. In the North the monasteries usually put their wealth to honest charitable uses which the local populations appreciated. But elsewhere a disproportionate amount of Church money seemed to be spent on display and self-indulgence, fostering not just jealousy but bitter anti-clericalism among the secular population.

For the Church not only possessed wealth which it consumed on objects far from pastoral, it also exacted money from the lay community. Tithe – payment of a proportion of personal income to the local priest – was a tax much more fiercely hated than royal levies to pay for wars or defence – which were less frequent and more obviously justifiable. Compulsory payments to the Church upon the probate of wills and, more directly, the mortuary payments demanded even of the poorest before a body could be laid to rest in the churchyard, stirred a sullen and venomous resentment which needed little to transform it into active hostility. And all these financial exactions were enforced by a system of Church courts which stood totally apart from the law of the land. To the ecclesiastical courts were summoned not only clerics, but any layman involved in matrimonial or testamentary disputes, or who came into conflict with the financial demands of the Church. From the sentence of the ecclesiastical courts there was no appeal to the law of the land, even when the ecclesiastical judgment appeared to contradict secular law. And any priest liable to prosecution in a secular court could automatically have his case transferred to clerical jurisdiction to be judged by his friends and colleagues. This special privilege – which rankled with the laity for obvious reasons – was called Benefit of Clergy.

Of course, there was nothing new in all this. Clerics had enjoyed special privileges for centuries, indeed they had fought for and won their rights when lay rulers were attempting to hinder their religious work. But, whatever justification there had once been for the power, wealth and privilege which made the Church effectively an *imperium in imperio* – a State within a State – many Englishmen at the beginning of the sixteenth century found it difficult to see what religious function many clerics fulfilled. Rare was the monk or friar who appeared truly inspired by spiritual vocation. Virulent diatribes were published

Popular anti-papal woodcut, showing the Pope as Antichrist 'inspired' by the breath of devils, while more devils reduce monks in a vat.

condemning the clergy as so many parasites gorging themselves at the expense of the body politic. Priests were not only neglecting their spiritual duties, said their critics – who were far from irreligious – but the clergy was also becoming so corrupt that the devout life was falling into disrepute.

Anti-clerical feeling was boiling up all through the 1520s and the fall of Wolsey removed a major obstacle to its free expression. Many had echoed Suffolk when he had clapped his fist on Campeggio's table and complained that times had been merry in England before there were cardinals. Throughout 1529 Londoners read eagerly Simon Fish's *A Supplication for the Beggars*, a bitter attack on greedy overfed clerics.

And then, as if on cue – and Henry certainly read Fish's diatribe – the King appointed as Chancellor not a cleric or even an ordinary layman, but the radical author of *Utopia*, which Dr Scarisbrick rightly describes as being in its day 'the most shocking book yet written in the English language'. We now know Sir Thomas More as a devout martyr for the cause of orthodoxy, but the very piety which later inspired the 'man for all seasons' to lay his head on the block had previously led him, like Erasmus, to criticise the priestly establishment as a Christian radical. More was not afraid to point out the contradiction between spiritual purity and worldly glory which priests like Wolsey embodied, and this gave him an anti-clerical reputation which, though it did no justice to the true profundity or complexity of his beliefs, meant that his promotion to the Chancellorship was taken as a sign of a new direction in royal policy towards the Church.

And finally, in the same autumn that More replaced Wolsey, Henry let slip the dogs of war and summoned a Parliament whose anti-clerical sentiments he certainly did not intend to muzzle. If the Pope wanted to assert ecclesiastical authority by summoning the King of England to Rome, Henry would show him just how much that authority really counted for. Anti-clericalism needed royal assistance if it was to become a meaningful force – and now the King needed anti-clericalism for his own ends. It was a marriage of convenience which was to yield offspring neither partner dreamt of. English history was about to turn a corner as significant as any it had negotiated before – or has encountered since.

5
The Breach
with Rome
1529-32

ONE AUTUMN EVENING, in October 1529, just after Henry VIII had finished dinner, he had the most remarkable conversation with Eustace Chapuys, the new ambassador whom the Emperor Charles had sent to handle the increasingly complicated relations between England and the Holy Roman Empire. That conversation shows not only the style of tactics that Henry was assuming *vis-à-vis* Catherine's European supporters and the Papacy, but also the direction his own ideas were taking. Would to God, he said, that the Pope and all his cardinals could set aside their worldly pomp and live according to the simple precepts of primitive Christianity. Their self-glorification had made for discord, scandal and heresy. Martin Luther was quite right to attack the vices and corruption of the clergy. Indeed, if the German had restricted his reforming zeal to those particular abuses, Henry would have taken up the pen in 1521 not to attack his opinions but to endorse them heartily. There certainly was heresy in the work of Luther, but that should not be allowed to conceal the very many great truths that this German zealot had brought to light. The Roman Church was in obvious need of reform and the Emperor Charles should do something about it. Henry himself certainly intended to do something about it in his own domains. He would make his own small contribution to the cleansing of the body of Christ and would set the English Church firmly in order. He would take up arms against the scandal of clerical corruption—and he concluded with a truly revolutionary remark: the only special power which the clergy possessed over laymen, he said stoutly, was absolution. Even the power of the Pope was very limited.

These were dangerous, novel sentiments. No longer was Henry elevating ecclesiastical power by giving the Pope the right to pronounce upon his marriage. He was attributing to himself the very power for which emperors had fought unsuccessfully great wars throughout the Middle Ages to claim, the right to pronounce judgment upon the Papacy and, if necessary, to intervene actively in ecclesiastical affairs.

As yet no one knew where such ideas might lead, but notions of an authority spiritual and temporal, such as England had never known, concentrated in one man's hands, were clearly germinating in the mind of the King. He would not hesitate to

William Warham,
Archbishop of Canterbury
from 1504 to 1532.
Drawing by Holbein.

put them into practice, should the Pope remain obdurate and force him to take action.

At all events, when Parliament met in 1529, it played exactly the game Henry wanted. Scarcely had the session opened than the Commons sent a long petition to the King. They demanded to know exactly what 'laws of God and the Holy Church' licensed clerics to buy and sell for gain, possess worldly goods, hold worldly jobs, occupy more than one position which was supposed to involve the pastoral care of souls, or to live far away from the parishes and sees where they had spiritual responsibilities.

The bishops sitting in the House of Lords were, needless to say, highly alarmed by this aggressive start to the Parliament. When they saw the Commons' petition they 'frowned and grunted'. They were even more alarmed when Henry allowed the Commons to put their anti-clerical programme into three bills which were passed on for the Lords' agreement. The bishops 'would in no wise consent', until Henry intervened personally and summoned eight members from each house to the Star Chamber to 'intercommune'. The bishops gave way –a weak-kneed performance which demonstrated how fiercely they felt the tide to be running against them. The bills became acts, and within weeks clerics guilty of non-residence, pluralism or engaging in commerce were appearing, not before ecclesiastical courts, but before the judges of the Exchequer. Worse, any layman who reported their misdemeanours, received part of the fine that the guilty cleric paid. Most significant of all, the power which Rome claimed to 'dispense' or forgive clerics who held more than one benefice was denied. Any priest who appealed to Rome would be fined £20, and whatever the Pope might say would be ignored. It was strong medicine, and there were stronger doses to come.

'This man, I trow, has got the right sow by the ear'

But in 1529, of course, Henry's principal interest was still his divorce. In the summer of that year, while the King was made helpless by the transfer of his case to Rome, an obscure young don named Thomas Cranmer, eking out a living as a private tutor at Waltham, met Stephen Gardiner. Gardiner had been billeted in the house where Cranmer was employed because the Court, travelling briskly throughout the summer months to leave plague in its wake, had come briefly to Waltham. Young Cranmer suggested to Gardiner that Henry might collect from all the universities in Europe their learned opinion on the legitimacy of the King of England's marriage, and Gardiner not only passed the idea on but generously gave full credit to its source. Henry was delighted, and, declaring that this Cranmer had 'the right sow by the ear', summoned him to Court. In less than four years the poverty-stricken don was to become Archbishop of Canterbury – gaining the very position that Gardiner had hitherto seemed the most likely to inherit.

Royal agents rode into Oxford and Cambridge early in 1530, quite sure of the response they could count on, and nearly a dozen went off to the Continent, somewhat more apprehensively. They toured libraries and bookshops for tomes that could justify the royal thesis, interviewed bishops, professors, scripture scholars, Hebrew scholars, Canon Law experts, doctors of medicine, friars, laymen – and even rabbis. No favourable opinion was disregarded. They whipped together special seminars at universities to pass resolutions in Henry's favour, and even despatched home from Venice two Hebrew scholars, one of whom, Marco Raphael, was a converted Jew who, in addition to supporting the King of England's cause, was famous for having invented a new type of invisible ink. The Sorbonne came out for Henry – but along with only five other Continental universities, and so, of course, did Oxford and Cambridge, though not without a certain amount of protest from their townspeople. Angry Oxford women stoned one poor agent they caught injudiciously immobilised relieving himself against the town wall.

A major difficulty was the fact that whatever Henry's two treasured texts from Leviticus said, they seemed at face value to be concerned with the way in which brothers should conduct themselves with sisters-in-law whose husbands were still *living*, and the proper attitude towards *dead* brothers' wives was set out in Deuteronomy chapter xv, verse 5: 'When brethren dwell together, and one of them dieth without children, the wife of the deceased shall not marry to another; but his brother shall take her, and raise up seed for his brother.' Which was exactly what Henry had done, providing a difficult hurdle for the most pro-English of European scholars to overcome. And there was an even more formidable obstacle to Cranmer's bright idea – the Pope himself. It was not long before strange Englishmen arrived in northern Italy doling out handsome sums of money to anyone who cared to satisfy their allegedly academic interests in the contradictory texts of Leviticus and Deuteronomy, and Clement understood immediately. The word went out from Rome, and the consequences were rapid. One Franciscan tried to give back to the English agents the money he had received. A papal nuncio tracked down a friar who had prepared a list of names favourable to Henry's cause, snatched the document from him and threw it into a fire. And then on 21 March 1530 Clement issued a bull formally prohibiting individuals from writing or speaking against the King of England's marriage to Queen Catherine. Henry's eight favourable judgments were useless.

Playing the papal game was becoming more and more pointless. Gathering together the opinions of Europe's academics had not been a means of denying Rome's authority to judge the divorce, but a method of collecting more evidence from which the Pope could make a decision. By the end of 1530, Henry was warning his ambassadors in Rome that in paying too assiduous a suit to Clement, they might 'acknowledge and grant so much of the Pope's jurisdiction, power, authority and laws as we should thereby preclude ourself from such remedy as we may attain here at home'.

He devised for his representatives in Rome a task yet more difficult and outlandish than any duty he had set them to date. They were to sneak into the Vatican library itself and there seek out any documents that proved the King of England's independence. Henry was becoming, as usual, so convinced of the justice of his cause that he was certain that evidence must exist to corroborate it. In fact, of course, there were no such documents and the ambassadors had finally to write to Henry that far from unearthing bulls which justified his new claims, they could only discover reiterations that confirmed the Pope's old-established authority over such matters.

But searching the Vatican archive was, fortunately for Henry, not the only string in the English bow. At Michaelmas 1530 fifteen clerics, eight of them bishops, including Queen Catherine's champion, John Fisher of Rochester, were summoned to appear before the King's Bench, there to answer a charge of *praemunire*. Henry was now indeed flexing his muscles, for the writ of *praemunire facias* was an obscure, little-used weapon turned against clerics who were alleged to have paid allegiance to Rome to the detriment of their allegiance to the King. The legislation under which the writ was issued was old, dating from disputes between Crown and Church in the fourteenth century. It was most effective for the darkness of its threats and the deliberate vagueness of its provisions which could mean that, in theory, every priest was liable to its heavy sanctions – forfeiture of property and imprisonment at the discretion of King and Council.

Such a writ had been issued against Wolsey after his fall; yet Henry had encouraged the Cardinal to build up his powers of papal origin, just as he knew well, as a pious Catholic, that all

English clerics owed their spiritual authority to the Pope. At what point did that debt prejudice the loyalty they owed to the King? *Praemunire* did not really say – or rather, it allowed the King to say and to act as both prosecutor and judge. It laid down fierce penalties which Henry could invoke whenever he himself was of the opinion that the mysterious point of no return had been reached. If he wished he could issue *praemunire* writs against every single priest in England – and that grandiose menace was far less implausible, though no less hypocritical and unfair, than it sounds.

By the end of 1530 the *praemunire* charges against the nine clerics cited at Michaelmas had indeed been extended to the whole English Church. In January 1531 the clergy were collectively charged with exercising their powers in the Church courts to the detriment of royal authority – and they offered no resistance. They pleaded guilty and were fined the magnificent sum of £100,000. Emboldened by his easy success, Henry pushed for more. He summoned to his Council old Warham, who could never have guessed when he withdrew from political affairs over a decade previously that his declining years would be so harassed and disturbed. The King demanded a more humble apology than the clergy had so far made, and also, much more significantly, ordered that he was no longer to be styled simply King and Defender of the Faith, but also 'protector and only supreme head of the English Church' – with an acknowledged responsibility for 'cure of souls'. Henry's Caesaropapism was actively on the march; he was now working up a momentum whose direction he may not fully have realised, but whose force was exhilarating.

'Protector and only supreme head of the English Church'

Unfortunately, however, all his threats were not bringing his divorce the slightest bit closer to realisation. Clement continued to insist in Rome that he must hear Catherine's side of the case, and Henry's representatives there had, consequently, had to play for time in the hope that some miracle might suddenly remove the stifling influence of the Emperor Charles. By 1532 Henry had been six long years nagging and worrying away at his heir-less marriage, and after all that time, frustration and expense his goal seemed as distant as ever. The deadlock was maddening – and there seemed no way out of it. If winning the Pope's friendship did not help, and threatening him did

The Great Seal of
Henry VIII.

not work, which way could Henry turn?

1532 was to provide the answer, for in that year a new man emerged to take over the direction of the King of England's 'Great Matter'. His name was Thomas Cromwell.

Thomas Cromwell was born in Putney around the year 1485 – just before the Tudors seized the throne of England for themselves. His father had a small business as a blacksmith and as a fuller – cleansing and thickening cloth. It was not the sort of enterprise to interest young Thomas, who went off, at an early age, to fight as a soldier of fortune in Italy. It was there, so his enemies later alleged, that he became intimate with the precepts of Machiavelli which guided his remarkable career to the private ear of Henry VIII. Cromwell himself liked to shock poor Cranmer with tales of his rascally youth, so different from the Archbishop's sheltered upbringing – Henry VIII liked rough diamonds.

Later Thomas set up for himself as a merchant with special connections with Antwerp, and, in London, he also gathered enough knowledge of the Common Law to become an attorney. Few early sixteenth-century Englishmen had had such a cosmopolitan and practical upbringing. Thomas Cromwell could speak several languages. And such was the character of the man that it is quite reasonable to assume that he groomed himself from an early age for the eminence and power he expected one day to enjoy. Certainly, to join, as he did in 1520, the household of Cardinal Wolsey showed a deliberate ambition. The Cardinal's household was at that time the effective government of England, and Cromwell became Wolsey's solicitor and general man of business. He worked hard – in his efficient and cool fashion – at making himself indispensable. When the Cardinal wished to perpetuate his memory with colleges in Ipswich and Oxford, the towns to whose educational facilities he owed so much, he set Cromwell the task of suppressing some twenty-nine religious houses whose monastic inhabitants were, allegedly, disgracefully un-monastic, and whose endowments were certainly suf-ficiently substantial to finance glorious monuments to the Cardinal's name. Cromwell used the task to store up lessons for the future – not only in how to dissolve monasteries, but in how not to draw attention to one's former humbleness and newly-acquired pomp.

A stoutish, heavy-faced man with small eyes and a hard mouth that turned down at the corners, Cromwell sought for himself neither glory nor popularity – and certainly achieved little enough of the latter. He sought only to do his job with the maximum of efficiency – which seldom makes for endearing or compassionate human relationships. And his origins made for loneliness among the lineage-conscious inhabitants of King Henry's Court. Wolsey and ministers before him had risen from humble birth, but they had all been churchmen. Cromwell was, in his personal career as in his historical achievement, an innovator, a man who rose to power by ability alone.

Thomas Cromwell was an unostentatious man who kept his own counsel, but some idea of his tastes can be gained from an inventory of his London home drawn up while he was still working for Wolsey, in 1527. The inventory also conveys an insight into the character of Henrician middle-class homes in general. In an age without institutional banks, Cromwell's rooms over-flowed with chests, for in the absence of cheque books or bank notes, how else could a man store and protect his

Modern Men and Modern Homes

The beginning of the sixteenth century saw important developments in domestic life. The great lords had mostly ceased to be semi-independent warrior barons in command of a military strength of their own, and were beginning their long decline into mere titled owners of large landed estates. Their homes thus no longer served as centres of military administration and, instead, factors of comfort, prestige and aesthetic design began to play increasingly greater roles. Great men began to build, decorate and furnish in a sumptuous manner, and as their lives became less peripatetic, their furniture and furnishings became fixed in the modern sense. All these developments are reflected by the type and style of furniture of the early Tudor period.

RIGHT The head of the bed which belonged to Anne Boleyn, with the royal arms of England. Despite its size and weight this would be carried from palace to palace during the progresses of the King and his Court.

ABOVE Illustration from Henry's psalter, showing the King seated on an X-chair, with his bed hung with draperies.
LEFT English oak arm-chair of the early sixteenth century.

113

Horham Hall, Essex, built
by Sir John Cutte,
Treasurer to the House-
hold of Henry VIII. It is a
fine example of a medium-
sized manor-house of the
period, with the Great Hall
running through the centre
of the house, lit by a
magnificent oriel window.

substance? In the room adjoining 'the new chamber' – like a
'good bourgeois' – Cromwell must have put some of his
freshly-acquired wealth into redecorations or alterations – the
inventory describes a great ship chest, bound with flat bars of
iron of Flanders work, all covered with yellow leather. In the
private chamber next to the hall was a huge round ship chest,
and there were at least two others, presumably also iron-bound
and locked – one of them in the old parlour.

There was no doubt, in 1528, whose man Thomas Cromwell
was, for this parlour was decorated with the arms of the Lord
Cardinal. Many Tudor Englishmen must have paid homage to
their master, whoever he was, in this fashion. Nor was the
householder's religious allegiance in doubt. The inventory lists
pious objects – two images in gilt leather of Our Lady and
St Christopher, a golden leather image of St Anthony under the
stairs – and the focal point of 'the new chamber' was a carved
and gilded altar of Our Lord's Nativity. Most Tudor households

114

said daily prayers, and to possess a fine altar or to employ a chaplain of your own implied social standing as well as religious devotion. In the kitchen were seven tall candlesticks and three little candlesticks set in wooden stocks – the house's flickering but portable lighting system. There was an iron toasting fork, a fine damask tablecloth with curious flowers and a diaper tablecloth sewn with a pattern of crossed diamonds.

The master of the house was not a flamboyant man, but his clothes were of solid quality: a furred gown, a gown trimmed with black damask and an old night gown faced with fox – sitting up in bed in a house heated only by coal fires could be a chilly business. Travelling, one needed protection as well, not only from the cold but from the rain and mud. So the Cromwell wardrobe contained a riding coat of brown and blue, welted with tawny velvet, a russet gown warmly lined with black lamb, an embroidered black gown for more ceremonial occasions – that went with a gilded sword and black velvet scabbard – a black satin hat, a riding cape and twelve pairs of gloves. Horse-riding in the sixteenth century was not a re-creation of the rich, it was a vital daily chore. Then there were the jewels – the neatest way of both displaying and storing wealth: eleven rings including a diamond, a rock ruby, an amethyst and a turquoise, all set in gold; eight pearls on a string, a diamond rose and, with inescapable piety, a golden *Agnus Dei* with an engraving of Our Lady and St George. The inventory shows a careful, thrifty man, not ostentatious in his wealth, but looking after himself and his own interests most comfortably – a selfishly sober forbear of Oliver Cromwell, to whom genealogists connect Thomas through the marriage of his sister Catherine to one Morgan Williams, a Putney brewer and alehouse keeper. The nature of this stolid – and far-sighted – Tudor Cromwell also came out in the difficult years that attended Wolsey's collapse.

When the Cardinal fell, Stephen Gardiner, his secretary, deserted him immediately. But Thomas Cromwell was not so hasty. He stayed with his old master until almost the end and that must be one reason why, three years later, he possessed the royal confidence which Gardiner could never attain and so fiercely envied both Cromwell and Cranmer for possessing. For Henry VIII could smell out loyalty and set great store by it despite – or perhaps because of – his own capacity for treachery and double-dealing. Cromwell acted as Wolsey's agent, keeping him in touch with events at the Court from which he was exiled, and carrying messages to and from the King. Thus the new man both kept faith with his past and built invaluable bridges for the future. He got himself hurriedly elected MP for Taunton, on the day before the 1529 Parliament met, and at the end of 1530 was sworn onto the Royal Council. By Christmas 1531 he was definitely one of the inner ring of royal advisers, and it can be no coincidence that in these months Henry's attitude towards the Pope and Church was becoming visibly firmer and more purposeful.

The relationship between Henry and the man who, by the beginning of 1533, was indubitably his chief minister, is even more subtle and intriguing than the partnership by which King and Cardinal had ruled England. For, after Wolsey, Henry never allowed himself to lose touch with the latest ebb and flow of events. He had, after all, between the Cardinal's fall and Cromwell's rise, governed England himself with some energy, even if he had lacked precise direction. That driving force continued and it was from his years with Cromwell that emerged the great triumphs of his reign: the successful outcome of the divorce, the achievement of royal control over the English Church and the rejection of papal authority, the elevation of English monarchical power to commanding heights it never held before or since, and the incredible treasure-trove looted from the monasteries.

That these achievements followed each other in a sequence so neat and logical that they now appear to us almost as parts of a pre-ordained programme can only be explained by the impact of Thomas Cromwell's systematic mind upon Henry's erratic energies. But these achievements, the great bundle of religious and political breakthroughs that historians have dubbed the Henrician Reformation, in fact articulated impulses and energies that had been bubbling away inside Henry for years. One of history's great 'ifs' is the question of how Henry would have resolved his problems if Thomas Cromwell had not shown him the way. He would not have acted so rapidly or efficiently, but it is not unreasonable to assume that, by the end of his reign, he would have reached – no matter how explosively

116

or painfully – the same position that he achieved so easily with Cromwell's help. Henry remained a lazy man, fond of his riding, tennis, and feasting, fitful in signing letters and bored with day-to-day administration, but during the great events of the 1530s he was far from being the absentee landlord of England. He worked in harness with Cromwell, fully in touch with important events, understanding every minute detail of policy when subtlety mattered, indulging himself fully in all his pleasures, yet remaining always and indisputably in control – as he demonstrated when, with the work completed, he struck his minister down.

But that did not happen until 1540. In the eight years before then, Cromwell set his own very precise stamp upon the reign of Henry VIII. Wolsey had little time for Parliaments; Cromwell gave the House of Commons, of which he was a member, a new importance – though not through any democratic motive but rather in the pursuit of sheer political effectiveness. It was Henry who had summoned Parliament, sensing its anti-clericalism and feeling sure it could help him in his quarrel with the Pope, but it was Cromwell who showed him how this assembly, which was to sit for seven years and earn its own special title, the Reformation Parliament, could turn English history in a new direction. The Supplication against the Ordinaries was the first gesture which shows Cromwell's guiding genius, for it picked up all the indiscriminate hostility to the clergy which Henry had fostered, and converted it from a rag-bag of grievances into part of the foundations of the royal supremacy in Church and State.

The Supplication probably had its origins in the first flush of anti-clericalism which marked the opening of the Reformation Parliament in 1529 after Wolsey's fall. It consisted of a long list of complaints, a somewhat rambling summary of everything the average layman found irritating about Church authority – the ecclesiastical fees, tithes, the use of excommunication by clergy as a weapon in their own private disputes and so on. Whatever its first inspiration, it was Cromwell who drafted it into the form in which, in 1532, it was presented to the King to be passed on to the clergy themselves. Now it took on a new character, for from its many common-place complaints, three were selected to be the subject of specific

'We thought that the clergy of our realm had been our subjects wholly, but now we have well perceived that they be but half our subjects'

117

Henry dining in his Privy Chamber: a sketch by Holbein. To the right is a sideboard used to display the royal plate.

reformation: that all future clerical legislation should receive the King's consent; that a special royal committee should have the power to look back over all past clerical legislation and either sanction or reject it for current use; and that all such legislation, past and present, should be deemed to derive its authority not from any clerical source but from the sovereignty of the King.

This was no fractious list of grievances: it represented a deliberate encroachment upon clerical power, and an addition to monarchical sovereignty. The clergy, sensing perhaps for the first time the true intention of Henry's attack on their power, naturally baulked. Archbishop Warham and Convocation

118

RIGHT Henry VIII's writing desk.
BELOW The King's lock, now at Hever Castle, which was taken from house to house during the royal progresses and was always used for the King's Bedchamber, so that absolute security could be assured.

Oak panel, carved with Tudor emblems, from Abbey House at Waltham Abbey. The house was leased to Sir Anthony Denny, a Privy Councillor and one of the King's favourite courtiers, at the time of the Dissolution of the Monasteries.

Holbein's drawing of a cup for Jane Seymour. Jane's motto 'Bound to obey and serve' is inscribed around the stem.

flatly rejected the royal demands. But that only gave Henry the very opening he needed. Summoning to his presence a delegation from Parliament, on 11 May 1532, the King melodramatically produced a copy of the oath of loyalty and obedience which all bishops swore to the Pope. Could it be, he mused ingenuously aloud, that the clergy were putting this oath to the Pope above the loyalty they owed to their King? 'Well-beloved subjects', he declaimed, 'we thought that the clergy of our realm had been our subjects wholly, but now we have well perceived that they be but half our subjects, yea, and scarce our subjects.'

This was the nub of the issue, yet whatever new allegiance Henry was demanding there was no doubt where the clergy's first loyalty traditionally lay, and it took the fiercest pressure to compel them to submit – after a fashion. Only three bishops fully agreed to the new powers the King was demanding. Two blankly refused, several consented with equivocal reservations, and eight were conveniently absent when the Convocation of southern clergy met to discuss the matter. It was scarcely a resounding victory for Henry – but nor could the Church congratulate itself too heartily. John Fisher of Rochester did not vote because he was genuinely ill – he was a fighter who would not have been scared to stand up and oppose the King. But the craven non-appearance of so many of the Church's upper hierarchy showed the calibre of the opposition Henry and Cromwell were up against, and the Submission of the Clergy of 15 May 1532 reflected little credit on the Roman Church in England.

The very next day Thomas More resigned the Chancellorship which he had with so much difficulty been persuaded to take up. Whatever reservations he had held in the past about Henry's attitude towards the Church and its precepts, he could no longer remain in a government which, increasingly under the influence of Cromwell, was obviously sharpening its swords for an all-out onslaught on everything that More held dear.

Earlier that year a bill had appeared in Parliament which not only proposed to cut off the fees (or *annates*) which all new English bishops paid to Rome when first appointed to their dioceses, but which also provided that bishops could be appointed without Rome being consulted. This was not sailing close to the wind, it was steering directly into it – though one clause made clear that, at this stage, English policy towards the Church still stemmed primarily from the political need to achieve a solution to the divorce. The act would not come into force for a year, and then it was Henry who would decide whether it should be put into effect or not. So if, in the meantime, Rome helped the King, then the flow of income from new English bishops would not be jeopardised. The act would only become effective if the Pope remained obstinate.

It was a none-too-subtle form of blackmail and Henry sent off a copy to the Pope and cardinals with the warning that though he, as their friend, was doing his best to subdue this sort of popular demand, his patience and his friendship could not endure for ever. Just what sort of friend to them the King of England really was, however, the Pope and cardinals deduced from reports that Henry, far from subduing the proposal to cut off *annates*, had gone down in person to Parliament on no less than three occasions in order to force the measure through in the face of fierce opposition from many lay members and, of course, from all the bishops as well as two abbots who also sat in the Lords.

The situation was still difficult. The King's Great Matter might now be in the hands of one of the most astute politicians England has ever known – but Thomas Cromwell alone was not enough. A shock had to be applied to the system, and this Henry and Anne Boleyn proceeded to do.

6
The King in his Splendour
1532-6

AFTER SIX YEARS of waiting, Anne Boleyn was more than a little bored with her nebulous position as the King's companion. For most of the time she was obliged to put up with Catherine's insistence that the original Queen was the true Queen – and had had to suffer Henry's confused compliance for the sake of public decency. To pacify Anne and to lend a certain respectability to the fact that through the summer of 1532 she had effectively appeared everywhere as his Queen, Henry bestowed upon her her first public mark of favour. She was created Marquess of Pembroke – *not* Marchioness, for she was given the title to hold in her own right – along with lands worth £1000 a year. It was an unconventional manœuvre. Now being styled 'Anne Rocheford', the new Marquess was given precedence over all other Marquesses. And her title was, in fact, the first ever to be created for a woman in her own right. Charles II was to dignify lady companions in a similar fashion but Henry VIII, as in matters religious, was breaking uncharted ground.

The King's Great Matter, for all its awe-inspiring political, theological and international ramifications, had sprung from one simple biological fact: Catherine's eventual failure to conceive. Now, at the end of 1532, the long years of expense and indecision were suddenly resolved with equal simplicity. Anne Boleyn became pregnant, and on 25 January 1533, she and Henry married secretly in a western turret of Wolsey's old palace of York Place, now called Whitehall.

The die was cast, there could be no going back. Henry VIII must now, willy-nilly, lead England into a decisively different future. And, now that the issue was reached, Henry acted with remarkable vigour, and, with Cromwell's help and a little good luck, with the most precise dexterity. His good fortune lay in the fact that the long hot summer of 1532 and the strains of fighting the King had proved too much for the aged Thomas Warham. He had died in August, leaving the see of Canterbury and the primacy of all England vacant. And to compound Henry's luck, Pope Clement had unpredictably, and despite all the King of England's recent threats, issued the bulls which sanctified the consecration of Warham's unlikely, not to say unsuitable successor, Thomas Cranmer. For though a pious and learned man, this mere archdeacon had scarcely enough pastoral

PREVIOUS PAGES Pen and ink design for a mural decoration at Nonsuch Palace.

126

experience to qualify him for the charge of a bishopric, let alone the entire English Church. The fact that it was Cranmer who had suggested the plan to organise European academic opinion in the King of England's favour was an obvious sign of where his sympathies lay.

The warning signs were all clearly there if Clement would read them, but he did not. Cranmer's appointment was assented to in February 1533, and in the very next month the bulls to consecrate him reached England. Within a fortnight the new Archbishop was summoning the King to explain why he had for twenty years been living in sin with his brother's wife. As Archbishop of Canterbury he must look into the 'great cause of matrimony, because much bruit exists among the common people on the subject'. The Gordian knot was to be cut in the manner Henry had first attempted in 1526, by the local judgment of his own tame cleric.

But six years had wrought a difference. Henry would not now appear before Cranmer as he had before Wolsey, a humble, ignorant layman placing everything in the hands of the all-powerful Church. The King wrote to Cranmer formally stating that he would bow to the Archbishop's decision as 'the

most principal minister of our spiritual jurisdiction within this
our realm'. But this would in no way alter the fact that Henry
was without superior on earth, that Cranmer exercised his
spiritual jurisdiction only 'by the sufferance of us and our
progenitors', and that Henry himself had, with God, ordained
Cranmer as Primate of all England. There was no mention at
all of the bulls of consecration Henry had been so keen to get
from the Pope.

With this constitutional brazenness went a new boldness on
the personal front. In February 1533, shortly after Henry and
Anne's secret marriage, but before Cranmer's bulls had arrived
from Rome, the Imperial ambassador was amazed by the
behaviour of the royal concubine:

> Without rhyme or reason amidst great company, as she came
> out of her chamber, [Anne Boleyn] began to say to one whom she
> loves well and who was formerly sent away from the court by the
> King out of jealousy [the poet, Sir Thomas Wyatt], that three days
> before she had had a furious hankering to eat apples, such as she
> had never had in her life before; and the King had told her that it
> was a sign she was pregnant; but she had said it was nothing of the
> sort. Then she burst out laughing loudly and returned to her room.
> Almost all the court heard what she said and did, and most of those
> present were much surprised and shocked.

They were not left to disapprove and gossip for long. Anne's
pregnancy and secret marriage were made public knowledge
and on 9 April 1533 a deputation led by the Dukes of Norfolk
and Suffolk rode out to Ampthill, where Queen Catherine was
living, effectively under house arrest. The Dukes told the
proud, lonely woman, who was now forty-eight years old with
streaks of grey in her rich auburn hair, that 'she need not trouble
any more about the King, for he had taken another wife and
that, in the future, she must abandon the title of Queen and be
called the "Princess-Dowager"', for she was the widow of the
King's dead brother. She would, of course, 'be left in possession
of her property', and if she gracefully acknowledged this new
state of affairs, promised Norfolk, then Henry would provide
for her 'more generously than she could expect' – though 'she
could hardly expect the King to support her and her household'.

Next month, on 10 May 1533, Cranmer opened his special
court. Wolsey had held his hearings in London. This time the

matter would be speedily dealt with far away from any possible commotion, at Dunstable, which was conveniently close to Catherine's place of captivity. Not that this mattered, in the event, for Catherine reiterated her insistence that she would be answerable only to the Pope in Rome and refused to have anything to do with any trumped-up tribunal Henry might devise. Cranmer's court duly declared her contumacious, as Campeggio's court had, but there the resemblance to that painfully rambling precedent ended. For after four neat sessions, on 23 May 1533, the Archbishop of Canterbury declared that Henry and Catherine had never been husband and wife. Cranmer then hurried to London where, in Lambeth Palace, with equal efficiency and promptness, he declared that the marriage between King Henry and Queen Anne was good and valid.

Within a week Anne Boleyn was crowned Queen. And on Saturday, 31 May 1533, on a day blessed with blue skies and sparkling sunshine, she tasted the victory she had fought so hard and waited so long to enjoy. 'She had added a panel to her skirts' – for the day of her *accouchement* was but four months off – but her long luxuriant black hair flowed down so long 'she could sit upon it in her litter'. She sailed down the River Thames, attended by a Cleopatra's fleet of barges, three hundred of them, all decked out in different coloured bunting and flags with bells that chimed and mingled with the music of minstrels and the boom of saluting cannon. Anne herself rode in poor Catherine's own barge with the old Queen's coats of arms hacked off to be replaced by her own. In Westminster Abbey Anne was anointed with holy coronation oil and on her head was placed, by the consecrated hands of the Archbishop of Canterbury, the crown of St Edward. It was a great triumph for her, a pregnant young woman of but middling birth. It was a still greater triumph for her husband, Henry VIII – King of England as never before.

Henry had, as usual, spent a fortune on the pageantry of Anne Boleyn's coronation. And he got, as usual, ostentatious value for money. But one significant ingredient was lacking from the celebrations. Wine flowing free in the streets had always, in the past, made for vocal and enthusiastic public participation. Yet

on this Whitsun holiday of 1533, the people of London were far from festive. 'How like you the look of the city, sweetheart?' Henry asked Anne. 'Sir, the city itself is well enow', replied Anne, 'but I saw so many caps on heads, and heard but few tongues.' The guilds had obediently performed their pageants, children had waved their flags and merchants had bowed. But few doffed their hats in respect to the new Queen, few cheered, and many boos were heard. The common rumour was that Anne had bewitched and seduced Henry with potions and love-philtres. Apprentices made fun of the way Henry's and Anne's initials were intertwined on the crimson and white arches of triumph, digging each other and crying 'HA! HA!' One witness heard a spectator denouncing Anne as a 'goggle-eyed whore' – so much for her legendary eyes. And another even more foolhardy soul called out 'God save Queen Catherine, our own righteous Queen'.

Anne Boleyn's lack of regality was noted scornfully, when she accepted a purse of gold from the merchants of Cheapside. 'As soon as she received the money, she placed it by her side in the litter, and thus she showed she was a person of low descent. For others remembered how when [Catherine] had passed for her coronation, she handed the money to the Captain of the Guard to be divided amongst the halberdiers and lackeys.'

There were significant gaps among the realm's worthies invited to be present. Several of the older nobility found excuses to keep them away – notably the great Earl of Shrewsbury. And Thomas More, though he knew it would anger the King, and though he was begged by his many friends not to heap coals on his own head, pointedly stayed at home in Chelsea.

The King's new marriage was far from popular. And never, in fact, at any stage in the Reformation, was there more than a small minority enthusiastically in favour of the religious changes that it brought to England. Henry VIII was racing dangerously ahead of his subjects' feeling. Within three years rebels would be raising the holy banner of Christ's Wounds to march against the King. Men like More and Fisher were prepared to go to the block for what they believed. Never, in the best part of the forty years for which Henry ruled, was his domestic position so precarious as it was during the early 1530s when he overthrew

Design for a triumphal
arch for use at Anne
Boleyn's coronation
procession in May 1533.
The sketch is possibly by
Holbein.

the faith Englishmen had followed for centuries, all, apparently, for the sake of a woman most Englishmen detested.

On the other hand, though England much detested Anne Boleyn and, strangely, loved the dour Iberian woman she replaced, men could appreciate the reasons of State which had impelled the King to take the course he did. Henry took personally his failure to engender a male heir. It rankled more and more as a reflection on his masculinity. The break with Rome was very much the gesture of a self-willed despot. But Henry's reluctance to leave England without a male successor was also a legitimate political anxiety his country shared.

After Anne's marriage and coronation many great statutes were passed by Thomas Cromwell through the Reformation Parliament which constructed for Henry – and his successors – a vast new dimension of royal authority: *The Act of Appeals* was the cornerstone of the edifice. 'This realm of England is an empire ...' declared its famous preamble, 'governed by one supreme Head and King.' The authority for this massive statement was vague. 'Divers sundry old authentic histories and chronicles' had, according to Cromwell, 'manifestly declared and expressed' that the King of England and no one else held 'plenary, whole and entire power, pre-eminence, authority, prerogative and jurisdiction' to decide matters both temporal and spiritual 'without the intermeddling of any exterior person.' The immediate object of the act was, obviously, to disqualify Catherine's appeal to Rome against Cranmer's annulment of her marriage to Henry. But its permanent effect, later confirmed by the more obviously titled *Act of Supremacy*, was to give Henry total control over the English Church. The other statutes added the practical details and provisions which flowed from this founding principle.

The Act of Dispensations dealt with the special licences which permitted departures from established Canon Law and Church practice. This had previously been a power which only Popes could exercise as, for example, when the young Henry had been granted a dispensation to marry his brother's widow. Now that Henry needed a new dispensation to marry the sister of a former mistress, Rome's authority was cut off. The only valid dispensations must, in future, originate in England.

135

The Act in Absolute Restraint of Annates turned into practical law the threat that Henry had made in 1532. All the payments that bishops had, on their appointment, traditionally paid to Rome, would now go to the Crown, and it would be the Crown, of course, which in the future held ultimate authority in the appointment of bishops.

The Act for the Submission of the Clergy put into statutory form the English Church's surrender of 1532. Not only were the clergy prevented from appealing to Rome, but their separate jurisdiction within England itself was, by this act, brought under the control of the ordinary law of the land.

The Act of First Fruits and Tenths annexed the first fruits of bishoprics to the Crown, extending this exaction to all spiritual benefices. In addition, the act demanded a tenth of their net incomes as a fixed annual tax, beginning at Christmas 1535. *The Treason Act* made it treasonable to declare the King a heretic or usurper, thus denying the authority of the Pope, even though the new English Church retained orthodox Catholic dogma.

The Act of Succession finally laid down the revised precedence of dynastic inheritance which, back in the 1520s, had been the mainspring of the whole break from Rome. Catherine's child Mary was declared illegitimate and the children of Henry and Anne became the true heirs to the throne. And this act, furthermore, proposed an oath to round off the whole package of legislation to make sure not only that Parliament approved it, but that the nation accepted the new order. As a test of political obedience men of prominence would be required to swear loyalty to the new succession and also to the royal supremacy in the Church.

These statutes added up to a true revolution, accomplished, largely thanks to Thomas Cromwell, in a matter of months. Yet there are some things that the most competent of mortal men cannot bring to pass, and the crowning piece of the whole great edifice, indeed the object, of all Henry's and Cromwell's toil and trouble, remained out of grasp. For when her time was accomplished, Anne Boleyn did not produce the longed-for male heir whose advent was to set the seal of divine approval on Henry's grand enterprise. Shortly before four o'clock on a Sunday afternoon, 7 September 1533, at Greenwich, she was delivered of a healthy, bouncing, delightful baby girl.

The following Wednesday the Lord Mayor and aldermen in their robes, chains and ermine came down river to see the new baby christened by the Bishop of London in the Church of the Franciscans at Greenwich. It was an impressive little ceremony – but Henry was not there. Nor were there any bonfires in the streets that night. Anne Boleyn's baby girl did not harmonise with King Henry's grand design. Indeed, she came dangerously close to making a mockery of it. And there were other real life complications which detracted from the glory of the great constitutional edifice Cromwell was constructing to elevate his King's power. It was one thing painlessly to pass laws as to what men should believe. It was another thing to get men to alter their beliefs, or, in some cases, to contradict principles they had always held dear.

The earliest trouble came from a woman, a simple nun from Canterbury. Elizabeth Barton, the 'Holy Maid of Kent' had, some time back, become celebrated all over England when she was miraculously cured in public of a disease from which she had long suffered. Already she had threatened Henry with the most dire consequences if he continued his attempt to divest himself of Catherine of Aragon. Now she became the centre of a group of devotees in Canterbury who applauded her prophesies: should Henry dare to marry Anne Boleyn he would cease to be King within a month and would die a villain's death; a letter of gold, sent down from Mary Magdalene in Heaven, was produced as divine endorsement of the Holy Maid's powers.

Opponents of the divorce, like Bishop Fisher of Rochester, the Carthusian Monks of London and the nun's spiritual director, Dr Edward Bocking, were pious men who believed in this sort of manifestation. Serious trouble had in the past been founded on less – indeed, the Maid's sex, courage and fame made her appear, more and more, a domestic Joan of Arc. And after Anne Boleyn's failure to bear a son Henry's patience was wearing thin. In November 1533 the worthies of the land, a novel collection of judges, nobles and Councillors, were assembled to debate for no less than three days the affair of the Holy Maid of Kent. Henry wanted her executed as both a heretic and a traitor, and saw in her destruction a weapon for striking at even more eminent opponents of his plans. But the

'God of his infinite goodness send prosperous life ... to the high and mighty Princess of England, Elizabeth'

Maid was the stuff by which popular movements are inspired. So later that month, in the cold winter of 1533, she was paraded with her Canterbury disciples on a scaffold outside St Paul's – not to be executed, but simply as a figure of public ridicule – while a government sermon denouncing her as a fraud and a harlot showed how Henry and Cromwell, in fact, took her much more seriously than that. She was sent back to prison until things had quietened down and then, in April of 1534 the affair ended at Tyburn. The Maid, her spiritual director Dr Bocking, and four others were hanged.

Henry had tried to implicate Bishop Fisher in the trouble Elizabeth Barton had caused, but the evidence of a major conspiracy was too thin. The King was anxious too, to strike at Thomas More, but the 'man for all seasons', not yet quite confident enough to speak plainly, or judging, perhaps, that the Maid's somewhat hysterical ravings were not the principle on which to stick, disowned Elizabeth as a 'lewd nun' and 'wicked woman'. Yet neither Fisher nor More, international figures before the divorce, and now becoming more and more the objects of European attention as they refused to swim with the English tide, could hope to escape Henry's wrath for ever. It was no longer enough to abstain from the great debate – as Thomas More wished to do and had, indeed, once been promised by Henry that he could. These men must now stand positively for the King or else be counted his enemies – and traitors.

John Fisher, indeed, was already treading very dangerous ground. In 1533 he sent a secret appeal to the Emperor Charles to use force against Henry – a desperate, directly treasonable initiative to take. But Fisher was not a man for half measures. Thomas More might equivocate, but John Fisher was not a modern man. He would eat alone in his great draughty palace at Rochester with only a skull for company on his table, while a priest read Gregorian homilies to him. Next to his skin he constantly wore a hair shirt, while beneath the red linen of the counterpane on his bed was hard canvas. For a mattress he had a bare straw mat. He was not a Court ecclesiastic, a bishop who loved to mingle with the mighty. For thirty years he had ridden round Kent, caring for his flock, leading them humbly through the liturgies and devotions of the medieval faith. 'Now be many

John Fisher, Bishop of Rochester: drawing by Holbein.

chalices of gold', he had written, 'but almost no golden priests.' 'Truly', wrote one of his admirers, 'of all the bishops that we have known or heard of in our days, it may best be said that this bishop hath well lived, and well and truly lurked: for who at any time hath seen him idle walk or wander?' He had not been afraid openly and vehemently to take Queen Catherine's part. Now, in the spring of 1534, he had to face the consequences. He was brought from Rochester to London and at Eastertide the gates of the Tower were shut behind him.

The very next day Sir Thomas More followed him. He had been summoned to appear before the Archbishop of Canterbury at Lambeth Palace on 13 April 1534, the day after the Maid of

Kent and her companions had suffered traitors' deaths at
Tyburn. As he left his beautiful red brick home set among the
fields and orchards of Chelsea – the home Erasmus had called
a 'Plato's Academy' – he felt a presentiment that he would never
see it again. For weeks his family and friends had been begging
him to swear the oath to the new succession, so More, to avoid
a scene, insisted that they should all remain in the house and not
accompany him to the river's edge, where the boat to take him
to Lambeth was awaiting him. He had with him only his
son-in-law, William Roper, who later recalled how sad and
quiet the former Lord Chancellor seemed. Then More suddenly
and inexplicably smiled. 'Son Roper', he said, 'I thank the Lord
the field is won.'

He refused absolutely Cranmer's gentle, anxious blandish-
ments to swear the oath that could save his life. He would swear
to the new succession, for that was something Parliaments were
empowered to alter and decide – even John Fisher would agree
to that. But to swear to the the supremacy of the King over the
Roman Church in England was something his conscience could
not allow. Cranmer thought that an oath to the succession alone
might be enough. He was not a man to see blood shed, and tried
to persuade Henry to let More and Fisher survive in this way.
But the King's anger was roused. The time for compromise
had passed; Anne's daughter had put Henry dangerously out
of humour and to the Tower More must go.

He spent over a year there – like Fisher – while ceaseless
commissions and deputations came and went, trying to sway
the voices of the two men whose assent came to represent some
almost divine – but unattainable – blessing on the new régime.
Henry tried everything – both threats and professions of deep
affection. He was anxious, he said, through Cromwell, 'to see
More in the world again'. But his prisoner knew just how
political that anxiety was. And it was politics – foreign politics –
which finally brought the two martyrs to the block.

In September 1534, eighteen months after Henry's marriage
to Anne and a year after the birth of the Princess Elizabeth,
Pope Clement had died, having finally given judgment – for
Catherine and against Henry, though without punishing Henry
for so flagrantly ignoring this decision. And Clement also
departed the world without taking the King of England to task

140

for all the monstrous incursions he was making into ecclesiastic authority. Henry had been threatened with excommunication, but it was never definitively promulgated. Many foreign critics at the time – and many historians since – have attacked the spinelessness of the English clergy in not fighting more against Henry and for the Pope – Fisher was the only bishop to die for the sake of Rome. But, in fact, it was the Pope who proved spineless and Rome who deserted the English clergy in its hour of need, rather than *vice versa*, by giving no solid instructions or direction to pursue during the crucial years. As Henry and Cromwell processed statute after statute through Parliament, switching the revenues and authority of the Pope to the King, Rome's interests in London were left in the hands of an in-effective nuncio, the Baron del Burgo, who did little to warn Clement of the catastrophe that was occurring, and whose warnings were ignored when he did. Not until 1535 did Rome give any solid indication that she cared for, prayed for, or would fight for her lonely followers in England – and then she effectively destroyed her principal champions. For on 20 May 1535 Cardinal Farnese who, as Clement's successor, took the title of Pope Paul III, formally announced that the imprisoned Bishop of Rochester, John Fisher, had been made a Prince of the Roman Church – a Cardinal. It was Fisher's death warrant – and More's as well. Seething with fury, Henry declared that he would help the Pope bestow this honour on the traitor personally by sending Fisher's bleeding head to Rome to have the Cardinal's hat placed on it.

This was to be the scything time. Humble obstacles were the first to be struck down. On 4 May 1535 three Carthusian fathers, a Brigittine monk and John Hale, vicar of Iylesworth, were fixed to hurdles, dragged to Tyburn, hanged, cut down while still living, disembowelled, mutilated and quartered. When asked at their trial who they thought agreed with their opposition to the King's religious policy they had replied 'All good men!' And one of them told the jury, 'Even in this realm of England, though the smaller part hold with you, I am sure the larger part is at heart of our opinion, although outwardly, partly from fear, partly from hope, they profess to be yours.' To make sure that fear, if not hope, was duly impressed on all who might be contemplating resistance to Henry's religious

OPPOSITE Sir Thomas More: a portrait by Holbein.

The last three Queens of Henry VIII.

ABOVE LEFT Anne of Cleves, by Holbein. This is Holbein's copy of the famous portrait which he produced for Henry, and which so whetted the King's appetite that he chose Anne as his bride.

ABOVE RIGHT Catherine Howard, a miniature attributed to Holbein and dating from 1540-1.

RIGHT Catherine Parr, portrait by an unknown artist.

changes, the arm of one of the Carthusians was left hanging over the door of his monastery as a grisly reminder of what befell those who blocked the royal path. Another Carthusian, Sebastian Newdigate, an old sporting companion of Henry, was, with several monks of the Charterhouse, chained, fettered and loaded with lead in a London street. There they were left unfed, wallowing in their own filth and unable to stand upright until, after many days of agony, they died.

On 22 June 1535 John Fisher went to the scaffold. The last survivor of Henry VII's old Council, who had guided young Henry through his early years and had, indeed, been given special charge over the new King by young Henry's mother, this aged saint had spent a long cold winter in the Tower with but a handful of rags to cover his body. Starvation made him stagger as he approached the block, but there was an enthusiasm, a positive eagerness in his eyes. He had dressed carefully for what he described as his 'marriage day'. To lie decapitated was this Cardinal's triumph – and his headless body was indeed left lying, almost naked, in the open for a full day before it was buried at Barking Abbey. His head – skull-like even in life – was piked on London Bridge, but it did not stay there, for under cover of darkness a friend took it down. King Henry could have his triumph, but he could not gloat over it long.

Sir Thomas More was also to die. He had seen from his window in the Tower the Carthusians fixed to their hurdles to be dragged the long miles to Tyburn. 'Dost thou not see', he asked his weeping daughter, 'that these blessed fathers be now as cheerfully going to their deaths as bridegrooms to their marriage?' His daughter begged him to change his mind. 'Too late, daughter', he gently replied, 'I beseech our Lord that if I ever make such a change, it may be too late indeed.' Sir Thomas saw his immortal soul at stake. When Sir William Kingston, the Constable of the Tower, broke down weeping at the news that his prisoner was to be executed, More told him to 'be of good cheer. For I will pray for you and my good lady, your wife, that we may meet in Heaven together, where we shall be merry for ever and ever.' More's sentence had originally been the dreadful torture inflicted on the Carthusians, but Henry commuted it to simple execution. Informed of the royal mercy, More smiled. 'God forbid that the King should use any more such mercy to any of my friends.' On the scaffold itself he had trouble with the long white beard which, denied shaving implements, he had, perforce, grown in his damp Tower cell. He pushed it out from under his neck for 'it had never committed treason', and he welcomed his end. 'I die loyal to God and the King', he declared. 'But to God first of all.'

It was a signal defeat for Henry. Some time earlier the Duke of Norfolk, in one of the ever more desperate attempts to sway More round to the royal policy, had resorted to threats. 'The wrath of the King is death', he had warned. 'Is that all?' replied Sir Thomas quietly. 'Then in good faith, between your grace and me is but this, that I shall die today – and you shall die tomorrow.'

'If a lion knew his strength, it were hard for any man to rule him'

'If a lion knew his strength', Sir Thomas More had once said to Thomas Cromwell, 'it were hard for any man to rule him.' With the destruction of his principal opponents, Henry VIII had roared and hunted to cruel effect. And within a few months he claimed yet another victim. Exiled to the cold damp fens of East Anglia, Queen Catherine, on 7 January 1536, breathed her last. Some said, of course, that she had died of poison, but Henry's contribution to her death was more simple than that: neglect, deprivation, insults, scorn and, in the end, hatred. When the news of her death reached London, Henry and Anne dressed from head to toe in exultant yellow and celebrated the event with Mass, a banquet, dancing and jousting.

However, with Catherine of Aragon dead, the great breach with Rome had been, so far as its principal object was concerned, for nothing. In 1536 Henry VIII was no longer young but, at forty-four, far from being too old to sire a son – and totally rid of his barren first wife. There had been no need for him to overturn the entire English Church just to remarry – though he was well aware, of course, that there were other political dividends – and certainly no need to tie himself to Anne Boleyn, who appeared no more successful at producing male heirs than her predecessor. On 27 January 1536, the very day that Queen Catherine was buried below the altar steps of Peterborough, Anne Boleyn miscarried. She excused the accident by her shock at the news that Henry, jousting at Greenwich, had been knocked from his horse and had lain unconscious for over two hours. That fall had certainly been a dangerous one, and some historians have even argued that it inflicted on Henry brain damage from which he never recovered. But it was, so far as Henry was concerned, no excuse for Anne's catastrophe. Tudor medical science – or the lack of it – meant that one miscarriage might well be the first of an unbreakable series. Sir Thomas More had prophesied that Anne might 'spurn our heads off like footballs, but it will not be long 'ere her head will dance the like dance,' and he was right. On 19 May 1536, less than twelve months after More's death and less than six months after Catherine's, she was herself mounting the scaffold to meet her end.

Henry had fallen out of love with Anne almost as Elizabeth was born in September 1533. And by September of the following year the King had found another love. It was noted that he was paying great attention to one of Anne's ladies-in-waiting, Jane Seymour, a quiet modest girl from Wiltshire, the daughter of Sir John Seymour of Wolf Hall. Jane was most reluctant to have anything to do with the royal advances, refusing a purse of gold, returning Henry's letters unopened and making him promise that he would not speak with her except in the presence of others. Poor Cromwell was summarily ejected from his palace apartments so that Sir Edward Seymour, Jane's brother who was greatly to benefit from the royal favour shown to his sister, could move in and thus provide a suitably chaperoned and convenient spot for scandal-free meetings. But Jane's reticence, of course, only served, like Anne Boleyn's coyness, to influence Henry's desire the more, though, unlike Anne, Jane was acting naturally, not waging a carefully calculated campaign. She was, by almost all accounts, a mild straightforward girl with few enemies: 'full of goodness', not dazzlingly pretty; 'of middle stature and no great beauty', said Chapuys, 'so fair that one would call her rather pale than otherwise'. The nature of the girl was such that when she married Henry, one of her greatest concerns was to reconcile the King with his elder daughter, the Princess Mary. She was an even-tempered, welcome contrast to Anne, who was a scold, and was acknowledged as such by all. Back in 1531, long before she was secure as Henry's wife, or even as the Marquess of Pembroke, she 'was becoming more arrogant every day,

Sir Edward Seymour, Jane's ambitious and able brother, who became Earl of Hertford and later Duke of Somerset.

using words and authority towards the King of which he has several times complained to the Duke of Norfolk, saying that she was not like the Queen [Catherine] who never in her life used ill words to him'.

Moreover, when in 1534 Anne discovered that Henry was flirting with one of her ladies-in-waiting she threw fiercer rages than ever – it is easy to see why Queen Elizabeth developed her temper, with a termagant for a mother and Henry as a sire. He bluntly told Anne she must put up with his dalliance – as her betters had done before. And the threat implied by that cruel thrust became reality early in 1536. Thomas Cromwell was instructed to examine the grounds for a second royal divorce, and Bishop Stokesley of London, who had won promotion for his assistance to the first was now enlisted to participate in the second. Unfortunately neither Cromwell nor the earnest bishop

148

could find the slightest fault with Henry's marriage – except, of course, for his connection with the recently dead Catherine, and to have attempted to use that first broken marriage as grounds for breaking the second would have been a manoeuvre round which even Henry's flexible conscience could not have bent.

So fault must be found in Anne, and in the spring of 1536, on 24 April, Cromwell and Norfolk headed a secret commission charged with doing just that. Within a week they had drawn up the most impressive list of adulterous liaisons in which the Queen was alleged to have engaged. Among her lovers, said the commission, was her brother, Lord Rochford, and this incest, coupled with her multiple adulteries, clearly constituted treason. No statute said as much, and no constitutional lawyer then or since has been able to explain precisely how sexual indiscretion *per se*, however frequent or with whatever novel partners, is grounds for treason. But Henry obviously took the whole thing as the most mortal insult and, in the sixteenth century, the wrath of the Prince was death. Within a month Anne was on trial before a panel of twenty-six peers presided over by the Duke of Norfolk – her uncle – and she was, of course, found guilty by a unanimous verdict.

Trumped up though the charges were, and transparent though the motive behind them might have been, we should not, today, be too hasty in rejecting them out of hand. Anne was far from being a wide-eyed innocent. The selfish beauty which enslaved Henry's wilfulness for years had snared others too. She had definitely changed the tone of the Henrician Court. Catherine had been, at least to start with, an open, fresh-faced inspiration, a good match for Henry's outdoor enthusiasms. Court life in her time had been a straight-forward bluff sort of affair with the ladies enjoying themselves with lots of good, clean fun. But Anne Boleyn – after several years at the Court of Francis I – found this all rather tedious. It was no accident that her first liaison, before she caught Henry's eye, was with Sir Thomas Wyatt, the rakish young poet. With him she established a pattern of flirtation where ill-concealment was intentional, which the King soon imitated and which became the pattern for a new style of Court behaviour.

There is the well-known tale of how, when Anne Boleyn

was flirting with both Sir Thomas Wyatt and the King, the two rivals played bowls. Sir Thomas had snatched from Anne, in love play, a locket that hung from her pocket. Henry had also stolen a love pledge from her – a ring which he wore on his little finger. When the two men began arguing about who had won the last throw of their game Henry waved Anne's ring in Wyatt's face crying, with an obvious leer, 'I tell thee it is mine'. Wyatt took the King's point – and replied immediately: 'And if it may like your majesty to give me leave that I might measure it, I hope it will be mine.' Whereupon, with an equally obvious gesture, he stretched out Anne's locket chain to its full length and measured the distance between the bowls and the jack.

This was the sort of incident that the older generations, and men not at the Court, liked both to hear and to deprecate. Anne, already unpopular, was disliked for the way in which she cultivated gallant, almost erotic, public compliments. She was 'the stimulant to, and priestess of, [an] elaborate cult of courtly love', writes Dr Scarisbrick. '"Pastime in the Queen's Chamber", love-lyrics and music, dancing, tokens, sighs – these were the very stuff of a young, and probably flirtatious, queen's daily round.' Mark Smeaton, the Court musician, Sir Henry Norris, a professional courtier who was a long-established favourite of Henry, Francis Weston and William Brereton, both gentlemen of her Privy Chamber, these were her special intimates. They were seen often in her company, danced with her frequently and shared her secrets. At the May Day celebrations at Greenwich in 1536, Anne made much of dropping her handkerchief as a token of favour to a young jouster. Henry took it – or chose to take it – as confirmation of the findings of the secret tribunal which had met the previous week. Its allegations of adultery were obviously true. The men cited were rounded up, and Henry Norris was sent straight to the Tower. Anne followed next day.

Henry – and Cromwell – wasted no time. On May 12 Norris, Weston, Brereton and Smeaton were tried and condemned. Five days later they were executed and two days after that, on 19 May 1536, Anne herself went to the block. As a token of special favour, Henry agreed that she should not have to suffer the butchery of the axeman, and had, instead, brought over from St Omer an expert executioner who did the job cleanly with a sharp French sword. As Sir Thomas More might have remarked, that was gracious mercy of a sort that most people would be quite happy to go without.

Henry did not dress in yellow, as he had done to celebrate his previous wife's death. But his behaviour was scarcely less callous. The very moment he heard that his second wife was dead, he embarked on his barge to visit Jane Seymour. Next day he was betrothed to her, and before the end of the same month of May 1536 – at the start of which Anne Boleyn had been his Queen – he took Jane to be his wife. Only Mark Smeaton, under the threat of torture, had confessed to the charges brought against Anne's alleged lovers, and similar charges brought against Sir Thomas Wyatt and another courtier, Sir Richard Page, had had to be dropped for lack of even the most strained evidence – but never did Henry once show the slightest qualms or remorse at the savage rapidity with which he struck down his second spouse.

His main concern – as ever – was a male heir, and he wasted no time before trying to produce one with Jane Seymour. But the new Act of Succession showed that, now in his mid-forties, Henry was facing up to the realities of his age and record in the engendering of sons. He might not recover from his next fall in the lists. So, in addition to bastardising Anne's daughter Elizabeth, and conferring the succession on any offspring of his marriage with Jane Seymour, the Act contained a clause which took account of the previously unmentionable possibility: that Henry might die before a son was sired. In Section IV the King was given the most unusual power of being able to *appoint* his successor if he and Jane had no children. Who did Henry have in mind? Was it perhaps Henry Fitzroy, the Duke of Richmond, whom Henry had elevated from illegitimate obscurity and could elevate still further? If this was so, the hope was short-lived, for within a few weeks of the second Act of Succession being passed, Richmond died suddenly. Henry was well aware of the alarm this might cause, not to mention the opportunities for intrigue involving Mary and Elizabeth, now the only surviving heirs, so he ordered Norfolk to bury the body secretly. Instead of a royal coffin, young Richmond's body was wrapped in lead and hidden under a bundle of straw in a wagon that took it to Thetford. There Norfolk had the boy quietly buried.

A more probable, if apparently unlikely, candidate for Henry's nomination was his elder daughter, the Princess Mary. Although the first Act of Succession had made her illegitimate, and the second Act confirmed this while also bastardising Elizabeth, Section IX meant that Henry could, in the absence of a son, bestow the crown upon one of his daughters, if he wished. So this gave a special significance to the elaborate reconciliation between father and elder daughter that occurred shortly before the new Act became law. Mary had suffered while Anne Boleyn was alive. She had been compelled always to give precedence to the baby Elizabeth, had received carefully contrived snubs from those pleased to remind her of her mother's fate, and had been prevented from moving freely in public for fear she should be applauded by those loyal to the old Queen. She was banned from her father's presence and, far worse, from her mother's, so that the two women – Mary's twentieth birthday was in February 1536 – had to endure separately the pain and sadness of Catherine's disgrace and death. Mary fell ill herself, but was moved from palace to palace as a result of Henry's not ungrounded fear that she might try to escape to the Continent with the aid of the Emperor Charles.

After Henry's marriage to Jane – who was known to favour a reconciliation – Mary tried to see her father again, and Cromwell agreed to act as an intermediary. He was not always a soulless, calculating man acting only to his own advantage, for, as go-between, he suffered cruelly from the royal anger at Mary's refusal to take the Oath of Supremacy that More and Fisher had declined. And Henry also insisted that the proud Princess should make to him a complete submission which included an admission of her illegitimacy. If she had refused he would have sent her to the block, if necessary. But Mary, alone, ill and advised even by Chapuys to submit, humbly did everything her father demanded – though asking Chapuys at the same time, to secure special absolution from the Pope for having signed the royal document presented to her. She explained to His Holiness, and her conscience, that she had put her name to it without reading a word it said.

Mary had the sort of spirit Henry admired, for all the fury

ANNO · DNI · · 1 · 5 · 4 · 4 ·

LADI MARI DOVGHTER TO
THE MOST VERTVOVS PRINCE
KING HENRI THE EIGHT

THE AGE · OF XXVIII YERES

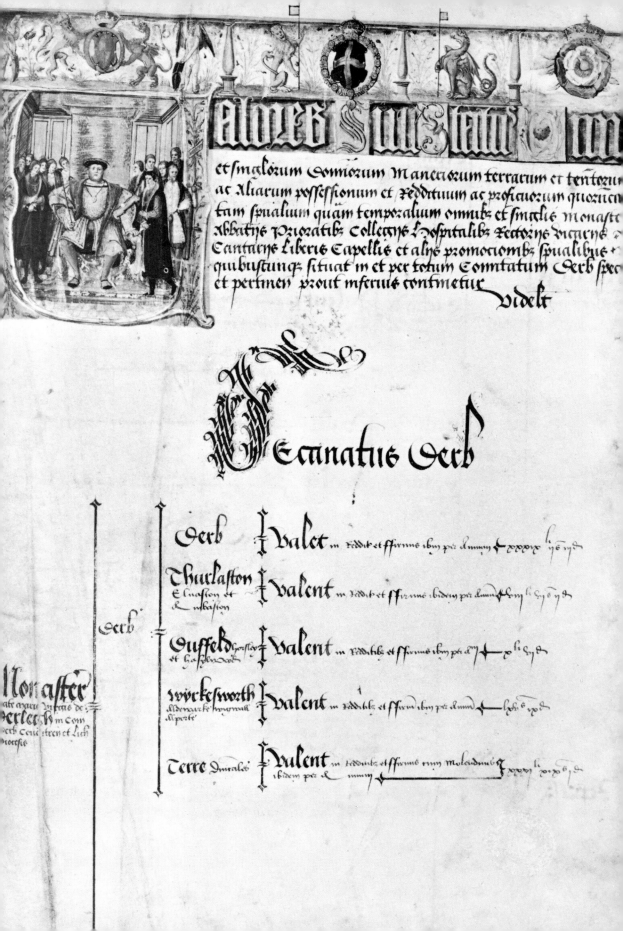

... et singulorum Comiciorum Maneriorum terrarium et tenetuum
ac aliarum possessionum et reddituum ac proficiorum quorumcum
tam spiritualium quam temporalium omnibus et singulis monaste
abbathijs Prioratibz Collegijs Hospitalibz Rectorijs Vicarijs
Cantarijs liberis Capellis et alijs promocionibz spiritualibz
quibuscumque situat in et per totum Comitatum Derb spec
et pertinen prout inferius continetur   videlicet

Decanatus Derb

Derb	Valet in reddit et firmis ibm per annum	£ xxxix li xs ijd
Thurlaston Elvaston et Ambaston	Valent in reddit et firmis ibidem per annum	£ xxxvj li xiij s vj d
Duffeld Horsley et Hassenhood	Valent in reddibz et firmis ibm per annum	£ xl li xiiij d
Wyrkesworth Aldenwarke hognall Alport	Valent in reddibz et firmis ibm per annum	£ lvj s viij d
Terre Dominicales	Valent in reddibz et firmis cum molendinis ibidem per annum	£ xxxvj li xix s vj d

Monasterij
... viris de
...lem in Com
Derb ... et Lich
...ocesis

which that spirit inspired when it obstructed his desires. He was pleased to have her back at Court with him, and, thanks to the benign influence of Jane Seymour, England had, at long last, a united royal family. Mary even played games with the baby Elizabeth.

After the terrible blood-lettings of the previous year Henry's religious changes seemed, at last, to be advancing smoothly – and profitably as well. The great rape of ecclesiastical land, generally known as the Dissolution of the Monasteries, was under way. That title describes, of course, exactly what occurred. The religious houses of England were closed down and their lands sold off – but the original object of the exercise was even more fundamental. In 1535 *Valor Ecclesiasticus*, a sort of Domesday Book of the entire wealth of the Church, had been drawn up under Cromwell's direction. It set out with remarkable detail and comprehensiveness the assets of the great corporation of which Henry was the new master, with its vast investments in buildings, jewellery, plate and land – a complex of wealth far larger than anything the State could boast of.

The long-standing historical controversy as to whether the monasteries in England really merited the harsh treatment they received at the hands of Henry VIII is a fruitless debate. Henry needed the money. After a quarter of a century of boundless extravagance he was having more than a little difficulty in meeting his commitments. Moreover the great of the land, as well as the not so great, had, as Chapuys noted, long cast covetous glances at the property of the monks. A share in the spoils of the attack on the Church was the price of their loyalty to the new order. Many monastic estates were, in any case, already leased out to yeomen and gentlemen, and they had long wanted complete ownership of lands they farmed on that basis. Now they could get it.

The very ease with which the monks gave in to the royal attack showed how monasticism as an ideal had lost its vigour in England. Truly pious men like More and Fisher did not shut themselves away from the world. And the social usefulness of the monasteries was very different from the image of folklore: friendly monks dispensing hospitality to poor travellers. It has been estimated that less than five per cent of monastic income

Title page of the *Valor Ecclesiasticus*, giving the valuations of ecclesiastical property in England and Wales. It was prepared under Cromwell's direction.

went to help the poor and needy. Few of the monasteries were truly charitable, tending to limit their hospitality to wealthy patrons and guests of honour – like Mary, Duchess of Suffolk, who often visited Butley Priory in Suffolk after hunting, to be regally entertained at a groaning board.

They were worldly men and women, these people behind monastic walls, often rushed into taking their vows when they were too young to understand their meaning. The visitors sent out in January 1535 had little difficulty in building up the case they were commissioned to construct, and Cromwell pronounced that dissolution was an urgent priority for monasteries with an income of less than £200 a year. Above this conveniently precise financial level monasteries magically became disciplined, vice-free institutions that the Supreme Head had no call to interfere with – the truth being of course that, not wanting to bite off more than he could chew, Cromwell had planned his appropriations in two stages: first the weaker houses, then, when his commissioners had more experience, the larger, wealthier institutions. And, in true Cromwell fashion, as he planned, so he executed. In February 1536 the bill to dissolve the smaller houses went before Parliament. Thereafter the richer plums were picked off at leisure – though, in the meantime, events occurred which at first threatened, and only in the long term made easier, the massive transfer of wealth from Church to State.

Henry's Reformation was a gamble. The industry and skill of Cromwell and the blustering of the King did not alter the fact that both men were skating on very thin ice. The country they ruled was a conservative one – as, indeed, was the whole world they lived in. In our own century, used to revolutions, changes in government policies and ideologies which sweep through entire social systems, it is difficult to envisage the shock of something like the Reformation which sought to change beliefs and habits unaltered for centuries. It was one thing for Henry to change queens or to execute recalcitrant members of the London-based establishment. That was a traditional royal prerogative. It was another matter when the changes consequent upon those measures started seeping down into towns and villages to alter loyalties and patterns of behaviour that seemed God-ordained and fixed for all time. Men became uneasy,

156

worried, resentful. Local jokes and gossip took on a vicious, spiteful, even treacherous tone. A Sussex man, hearing of Henry's terrible fall which had induced Anne Boleyn's miscarriage, said he was sorry the King had recovered: 'it were better he had broken his neck.' The 1530s were a difficult, testing time, when royal popularity reached a sadly low ebb. If Henry knew truly what his subjects thought about him, said one Kentish man, 'it would make his heart quake'.

The South of England restricted its discontent to rumours and complaints of the sort which government records have preserved for us to read today: alehouse brawls and arguments, indiscreet gossip on the village green. But the North was made of sterner stuff. It had always been – and was long to remain – virtually an independent country, owing allegiance to its own great lords, the Percies, the Darcies and so on – and to the King only as long as those lords so desired. Henry VIII had never visited the North and was only to pay it one short visit – which was one more than any of his Tudor successors managed. It was wild, rough, untamed territory, crucially important because of its border with Scotland, but mistrusted and feared like Wales and Ireland on account of its natives' truculent independence. Set in their ways, the Northerners were 'very ignorant and rude', complained one metropolitan Protestant, 'knowing not what true religion meant, but altogether nose led in superstition and popery'. They had no time for the new-fangled religion from the south, and in the summer of 1536, as Henry was revelling in the company of his third wife amid pageants and festivities whose extravagance was the greater for the prospect of the monastic confiscations that would pay for them, the wild North flared into widespread and multiple rebellion. Historians have dubbed the many-headed revolt the Pilgrimage of Grace, but in fact that title is properly reserved for just one of the risings – the outbreak which started on 8 October in Yorkshire under the leadership of Robert Aske.

One of the rebellions had been long planned by three great Northern lords – Thomas Darcy, John Hussey and Thomas Dacre – aided and abetted by Chapuys on behalf of Charles V. Their conspiracy had started as a plot forcibly to remove Catherine of Aragon from her difficulties, but had continued, after her death, to become a general assault upon Henry by

'Our king wants only an apple and a fair wench to dally with'

The Dissolution of the Monasteries

In 1536, Parliament passed an Act dissolving all small ecclesiastical foundations with an annual income of less than £200. In the next four years followed the dissolution of the wealthier houses. The King gained lands worth about £100,000 from this, but as he often sold off or leased the properties to his courtiers, he gained nearly £1,500,000 for the royal coffers. The Dissolution brought about far-reaching changes in almost every aspect of English life, and in the North these changes were to breed resentment and open dissension for the rest of the century.

RIGHT Fountains Abbey, one of the great Cistercian monasteries of Yorkshire. The foundation was dissolved in 1536, and the Abbot was deposed; he was later condemned to death for intriguing to regain his power.

LEFT Titchfield Abbey, Hampshire. The abbey lands were sold to Sir Thomas Wriothesley, later Earl of Southampton, one of Cromwell's protégés, whose career advanced rapidly in the 1530s. Wriothesley converted the medieval monastic buildings at Titchfield into a fine house, using the former monastic buildings as his quarry for stone.

RIGHT Nineteenth-century drawing of Much Wenlock Abbey, acquired by the Earl of Shrewsbury at the Dissolution of the Monasteries.

traditional Roman Catholics. But the mainspring of all the risings was deeper-rooted than aristocratic discontent. There was a basic, regional resentment at the encroaching power of the central government, for Cromwell's administrative revolution was bringing not just the Church, but the whole country more effectively under the thumb of royal authority. There were also economic grievances: general inflation meant rising rents, and attempts by landlords to make their lands more efficient meant unemployment; some landowners were extending their property by encroaching upon the common lands on which people had previously freely grazed their animals.

In this financially straitened context government taxation became particularly resented, and Cromwell had sent out commissioners in 1534 to raise a subsidy. Above all, welding these complaints, fairly minor in themselves, into indignation potent enough to inspire rebellion was religion. The attack on the monasteries had in 1536 hardly begun, but, on top of all the religious changes of the previous years, the arrival of Cromwell's commissioners to close down the monasteries in the one part of England where they retained a genuine social function and positive contact with local communities brought simmering resentments to boiling point.

A riot which broke out in Louth, Lincolnshire on 1 October 1536 spread rapidly across the whole county. The ringleaders demanded the dismissal of heretical bishops like Cranmer, an end to the dissolution of the great abbeys, and Cromwell delivered up for the people to do with him as they thought fit. The rapid mustering of an army under the Duke of Suffolk put paid to that particular movement. But the Lincolnshire rebels were still disbanding when news came of a far more serious rising in Yorkshire. The ringleader was a country gentleman and lawyer, Robert Aske, who marched under a banner showing Christ's bleeding wounds and who insisted that his movement was a Pilgrimage. Formal proposals to the government were drawn up at Pontefract in December – Henry simply did not possess the armed strength to attack the rebels – and these proposals, too, were religious in inspiration: Catherine's daughter Mary should be legitimised, the authority of the Pope should be restored and the Church should have returned to it the powers taken over by the State.

But the pious character of the Pilgrimage was its very un-doing, for though the Pontefract proposals embraced economic and political demands, including the calling of a Parliament not subservient to the royal will, Aske remained steadfastly loyal to Henry VIII – as his 'Oath of the Honourable Men' made clear:

> Ye shall not enter into this our Pilgrimage of Grace for the Commonwealth, but only for the love that ye do bear unto Almighty God his faith, and to Holy Church militant and the maintenance thereof, to the preservation of the king's person and his issue, to the purifying of the nobility, and to expulse all villein blood and evil counsellors against the Commonwealth from his Grace and his Privy Council of the same.

It was an old-fashioned, touching, traditional declaration. Aske would not countenance his followers' wish to march south to take London – as they might well have done; Henry was an autocrat, but the actual force at his disposal was, except after long preparations in time of war, negligible. The only sub-stantial royal army, rapidly thrown together under Suffolk's command, could not risk leaving the still turbulent towns of Lincolnshire. The Earls of Shrewsbury and Rutland were, on account of their lands in the area, proclaimed joint generals of the levies that should put down the Pilgrimage. But they were powerless. Dr Scarisbrick indeed believes that Henry VIII was, at this time, in the most crucial danger.

> The crown was scarcely in greater peril in 1588 [the year of the Spanish Armada] or 1642 [the outbreak of the Civil War] ... Had things been only slightly different [for Henry VIII] his Reformation might have been wholly or largely undone, Cromwell, Cranmer and the rest expelled, he himself destroyed and Mary brought to the throne ... sixteen years ahead of her time.

That none of this did, in fact, happen was not thanks to Henry. It was the fault of the rebels themselves – or rather of Robert Aske, in particular – the inspirational, naïve, one-eyed man who understood so well the character of Yorkshire and the Pilgrims he led, but who did not understand the true character of his King. He saved Henry VIII by trusting him, by believing the royal promise brought by the Duke of Norfolk of a Parliament, and a pardon for all the Pilgrims who went home in peace. Aske took off his badge, with its bleeding wounds of Christ, and promised that henceforth 'We will wear no badge or sign

'We will wear no badge or sign but the badge of our Sovereign Lord'

161

but the badge of our Sovereign Lord.' His Pilgrims also went home peacefully – and they kept their promise.

Henry, of course, did not – but events provided him with an excuse for breaking faith. One Francis Bigod, a strange young man who was a Protestant but who rebelled against Henry because of the religious powers that the King was assuming, declared that Aske's surrender was a betrayal. Aske and the Pilgrims might trust the royal word, but he did not. In January and February 1537 conspirators attempted to seize Hull and Scarborough: peasants from Cumberland and Westmorland laid siege to Carlisle. Aske and other moderate leaders called for restraint, but they were ignored – both by the rebels and by the King, for this was the pretext Henry had been waiting for. All through the troubles he had been issuing the most explosive threats: Lincolnshire he declared 'one of the most brute and beastly shires of the whole realm'; he promised the rebels 'the utter destruction of them, their wives and children'. Though compelled by Aske's strength to appear more conciliatory to the men of Yorkshire, he always intended bloody revenge – and now, in the beginning of 1537, he got it. The Earls of Shrewsbury and Rutland could move in at last. Some seventy Cumberland peasants were hanged in their villages, on trees in their gardens for their wives and children to see: the monks of Sawley, one of the monasteries re-opened by the Pilgrims, were 'hanged on long pieces of timber or otherwise out of the steeple'. Poor Aske, of course, was brought to London, condemned and then, with the other ringleaders, sent back up North to be executed in view of the people who had cheered him a few months earlier. And the Duke of Norfolk rode round on a Bloody Assize which claimed over one hundred and fifty victims, including one woman who was burned to death.

The Pilgrimage of Grace and the other disturbances gave Cromwell the very excuse he was looking for to dissolve the larger monastic institutions – while the men who had stood by Henry could now enjoy the rewards they had counted on. The Earl of Shrewsbury, for example, obtained the abbeys of Buildwas, Combermere, Shrewsbury, Welbeck and Wilton, as well as the priories of Tutbury and Wenlock. The Earl of Rutland, his co-general, received Beverley, Chartley, Croxton, Garradon, Nunbarnholme and that gem of all England's

'Hanged on long pieces of timber or otherwise out of the steeple'

abbeys, Rievaulx. By 1540 England's last religious house, the rich Augustinian abbey of Waltham, had been closed, the King's annual income was some fifty per cent larger, his lands were more extensive than ever before, and the loyalty of the establishment to the new order of things had been purchased and secured in a fashion that the toughest tests were to prove unshakable. And just to make quite sure that no further Pilgrimages should threaten the peace of the realm, Cromwell, in the summer of 1537, had a special Council of the North set up to rule firmly and permanently over the five wild Northern counties, strengthening at the same time the powers of the similar Council ruling over Wales. The royal authority was more solidly based than ever.

The great testing time of Henry VIII's reign was over. The King had come close to the destruction all Europe had predicted for him and had emerged triumphant. He had carried England through one of the great revolutions in her history – perhaps the greatest. He was powerful and rich as never before. His treatment of his Northern subjects showed he could be a fierce master, his rewards to his supporters showed he could be generous – and now Henry took steps to demonstrate as well the permanence of his power. Not only his contemporaries but also posterity should be witness to his magnificence. Some two thousand acres of prime Home Counties estate land were swept clean to make way for the greatest palace in England, a monument that could stand comparison with the finest in Europe – in the world for that matter – and which would bear a name to match – Nonsuch.

Henry had already made sure of a kind of eternity by constructing and embellishing buildings on a scale unmatched by any previous English monarch. After rebuilding the palace of Bridewell, he had set about a yet more ambitious project up-river in the city of Westminster. Cardinal Wolsey had turned the London residence of the archbishops of York, York Place, into a palace whose glory Henry envied keenly. York Place stood on the east side of modern Whitehall, near the old, decrepit palace of Westminster, and scarcely had the Cardinal fallen from grace than Henry made this residence his own – despite Wolsey's quite justified objection that it was not his own to be confiscated: it was in the perpetual possession of the

Whitehall Palace

York Place was the London residence of the archbishops of York. Wolsey had converted the medieval house into a splendid palace which Henry coveted. At the fall of the Cardinal Henry took over York Place and enlarged it into his great Palace of Whitehall to serve as a London home for Anne Boleyn. When he had completed his additions, Whitehall covered an area of twenty-three acres, stretching from Charing Cross to the old Palace of Westminster. He imported from the Continent craftsmen to embellish the buildings and created an appropriate setting for the Tudor monarchy.

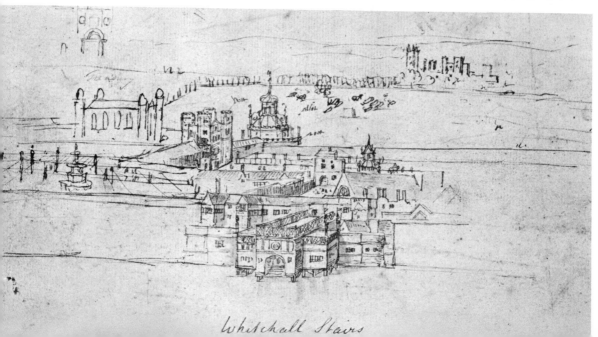

Whitehall Stairs

LEFT Detail from the painting of Henry VIII and his family showing part of the Palace of Whitehall The walls are covered in grotesque decorations, presumably in paint. The Palace was embellished inside and out with Henry's arms supported by royal beasts, and two of these have been portrayed in the picture, seated on columns.

RIGHT 'The Holbein Gate' at Whitehall, also known as the 'Cockpit Gate'. This gatehouse was built over the highway from Charing Cross to Westminster and was richly embellished with Henry's arms and symbols.

LEFT Anthony van Wyngaerde's drawing of Whitehall Palace, viewed from the Thames. Henry constructed a new embankment along the river at this point to prevent flooding, but the Whitehall Stairs continued to serve as a general landing stage, with public right of way through the Palace.

archbishopric of York to be occupied by its successive incumbents. But, unabashed, Henry masked the original proprietorship of his new palace by making sure it was referred to by the title employed to this day – Whitehall – and by adding to Wolsey's original residence a collection of gardens, galleries, yards, courts and gatehouses that rambled all over the area that we now describe by that name. It probably stretched into the area where Scottish royal visitors to London usually stayed – Scotland Yard – and westwards across the gardens where Charles II was to play Pall Mall and to construct an aviary (Birdcage Walk), to the leper hospital owned by Eton College and dedicated to St James. Here, in 1532, Henry began building a second London palace which – unlike Whitehall, destroyed by fire in 1697 – survives to show the twentieth century the stolid majesty of Henry VIII's architectural taste.

Hampton Court, the country house started by Wolsey only to be confiscated, like York Place, and altered by the King, displays the red brick self-confidence of Henrician architecture to even greater advantage. Between 1531 and 1536 Hampton Court's Great Hall was built, and so eager was Henry to see the completed splendour of the hammer-beamed roof that work went on round the clock, the night shift having their labours illuminated by candlelight. Wolsey's arms were replaced by Henry's shields and monograms and, as an even clearer stamp of the palace's new ownership, the fine Close Tennis Court was constructed.

But, in 1538 began the project to outdazzle them all, Nonsuch. This palace, six miles south-east of Hampton Court, was to be a veritable Versailles that involved destroying an entire village and its church. Hundreds of craftsmen were imported: woodcarvers and gilders from Italy, France and the Low Countries; six French clockmakers to erect the great clock; a posse of French gardeners to lay out paths, lawns, fountains – and two hundred pear trees brought from France. Henry's aim was obvious – to rival Francis I's country château of Chambord. But whereas that glittering memorial to Renaissance kingship has survived, Nonsuch has not – indeed it is difficult to discover any trace of it today.

Still, in the 1530s, England and Europe took the point that Henry was emphasising in bricks and mortar not only at

OPPOSITE The hammer-beamed roof of the Great Hall of Hampton Court, which was completed in 1536. Henry's emblems of the portcullis, the Tudor rose and the fleur-de-lys, and those of Anne Boleyn, can be seen on the hanging pendants and within the structure of the beams.

Section of the frieze and ceiling of Wolsey's Closet at Hampton Court. Wolsey brought over many craftsmen from France and the Low Countries to work on Hampton Court, and they may well have incorporated the Renaissance motifs into the decoration.

Bridewell, Whitehall, St James's, Hampton Court and Nonsuch, but also in embellishments around older palaces at Eltham, Windsor and Greenwich. In the autumn of 1537 came the triumph which lent still greater glory and permanence to this unrivalled explosion of construction and ornamentation. On 12 October 1537, Queen Jane Seymour, in the palace of Hampton Court, was delivered of a healthy baby son. England's ten-year battle with the Papacy was finally blessed with its intended result. More than a victory, it was a token of divine approval, news good enough to launch the most splendid

168

celebrations – and even to bring Henry VIII back from Esher, whither he had fled to avoid the risk of October plague. The boy would be called Edward, for that was the name of his great-grandfather and of the saint on whose holy day the news of his birth reached Henry. This legitimate male heir filled Henry's cup of joy to overflowing – and seems to have moved him, too, to a rare display of genuine compassion.

For poor Jane Seymour, ripped open by barbaric Tudor surgery for the sake of her son's life, lay ill with puerperal fever, and twelve days later she died. Cromwell, who was her friend,

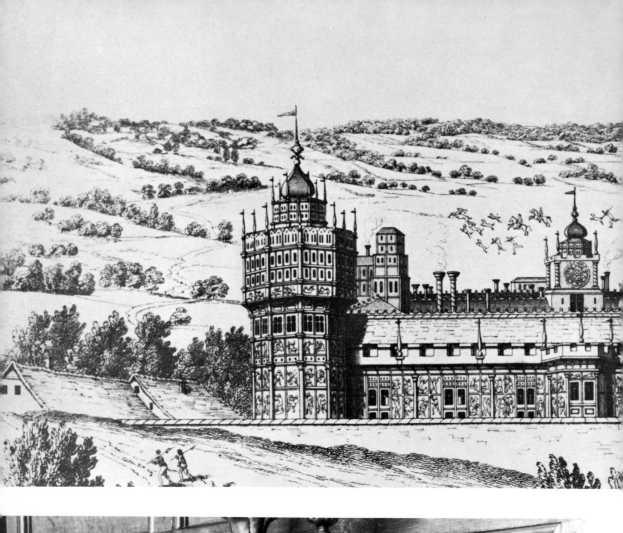

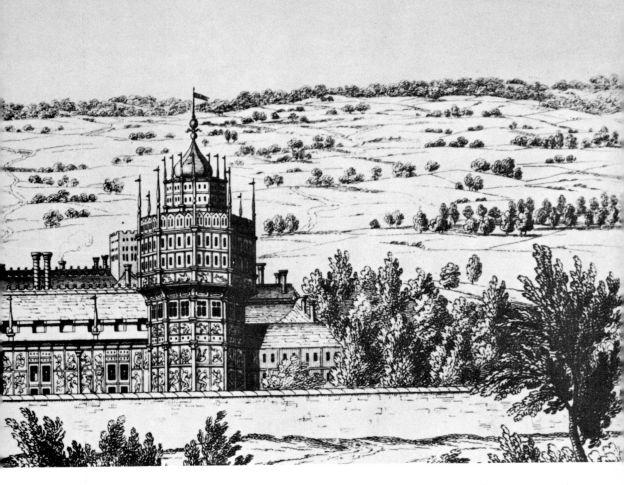

In 1538, Henry embarked upon his most ambitious building project, the Palace of Nonsuch in Surrey. With the help of Continental craftsmen, probably headed by Nicolas Bellin of Modena – who had worked at Fontainebleau – he created a palace of fantasy, in rivalry with Francis I's château at Chambord.
ABOVE Hoefnagel's drawing of Nonsuch, executed in the late sixteenth century.
LEFT Grotesque panels, decorated with the King's initials and emblems, from Nonsuch Palace, now in Loseley Park, Guildford.

said she had been the victim of those 'who suffered her to take great cold and to eat things that her fantasy called for'. Whatever the reason for her death, Henry's grief was massive and sincere. Quiet, modest Jane was lain in state for three weeks and then, alone of Henry's wives, she was buried in pomp and glory in St George's Chapel in Windsor. It has been said that her name was on Henry's lips as he died, and that she was the only one of his six wives that he truly loved. Certainly, his Will was to direct that he should be buried alongside this woman who had borne his son, and when Francis I sent his congratulations on the birth of Edward, the English King replied sadly 'Divine Providence hath mingled my joy with the bitterness of the death of her who brought me this happiness.' Diplomatic despatches are seldom to be taken at their face value, still less in the sixteenth century and less still when worded by Henry VIII. But in this case we might, perhaps, fairly give Henry the benefit of the doubt.

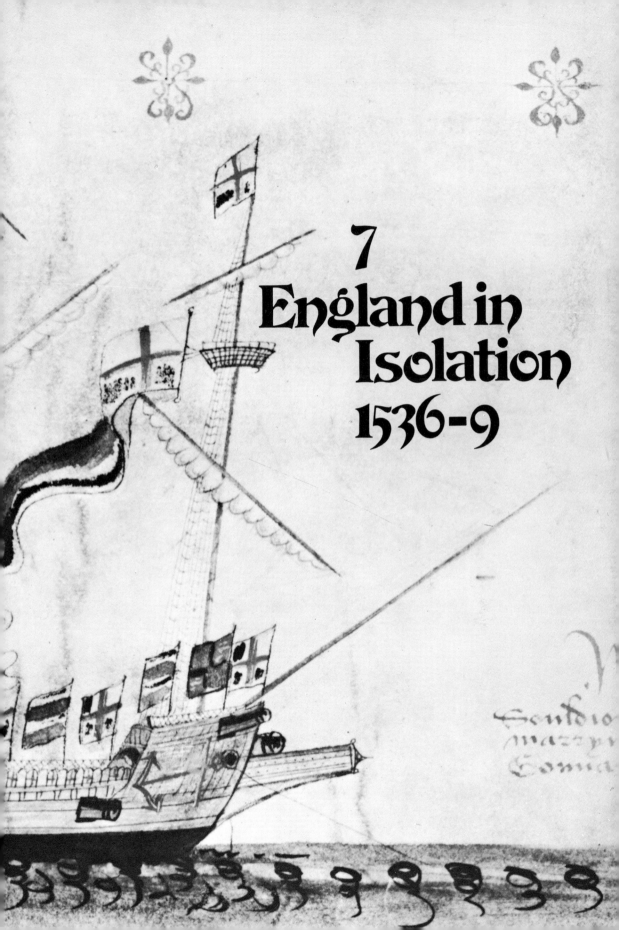

7
England in
Isolation
1536-9

HENRY SURVIVED Jane Seymour by less than ten years. And though this represented a quarter of the time that he ruled England, the final decade was very much a rounding off of his reign. Not even a rounding off, perhaps, so much as a rapidly repeated resumé of what he had done before. He had taken three wives, now he took three more. He had struck down Thomas Wolsey, now he struck down Thomas Cromwell. And he ended as he had begun – with a complicated, costly and pointless war.

Foreign affairs had not been at the centre of Henry's interest during the great Reformation years – but they had been no less tortuous than the intrigues and jostlings which had obsessed Wolsey. From the Cardinal Henry and Cromwell had inherited the alliance with France; but Francis I, as his most Catholic Majesty, theoretically one of the pillars of the Roman Church, was under strong pressure from the Pope not only to cease succouring the rebellious King of England, but also to undertake a crusade against him. England was fortunate that, all through the testing time of her Reformation, the Emperor Charles was embroiled with the Lutheran princes of Germany and with the ever more menacing Turks, and that furthermore in 1536, just as tensions were boiling up to the Pilgrimage of Grace and the other great rebellions against the Henrician settlement, Charles and Francis declared war on each other.

But in 1538 the King of France and the Emperor patched up their differences, and in that same year – not before time – Rome finally made effective retaliation for all the insults suffered at the hands of Henry VIII. A bull of deprivation, first drafted in 1535, now came into effect, calling upon Christians everywhere to attack and destroy the English King. Henry was declared deposed and his subjects absolved of all obedience to him. Cromwell decided that an urgent priority was to recruit at least one powerful ally for England abroad, and that a very good method of winning friends and influencing Europeans was to make Henry's fourth wife a foreign one. The minister felt his negotiating hand would be greatly strengthened if he could dangle before Europe's princes the prospect of marrying one of their daughters to the King of England – and Henry himself revelled in the prospect of being able to handpick his next spouse from the world's most beautiful princesses. Neither King nor minister seem to have worried unduly that Henry's

record when it came to wives – one divorced, one beheaded, one died – might well dampen the reciprocal enthusiasm of many young ladies, and their fathers.

The first approach was to France. Francis had a daughter, Margaret, while an equally tempting proposition was Marie, the daughter of the powerful Duke of Guise. She was being courted on behalf of young James v of Scotland, who had never proved the docile nephew his English uncle had hoped for, and whom Henry would have dearly loved to worst. Marie was, furthermore, the sort of mature, attractive, experienced widow that Henry fancied. He was, as he himself later explained, 'big in person and had need of a big wife'. But Henry's Scottish nephew frustrated his uncle's appetite for large limbs, negotiating secretly and sweeping Marie of Guise up to Edinburgh to marry her in May 1538. It was fortunate for James that in the meantime Henry's fancy had settled elsewhere, on Christina, the daughter of the deposed King of Denmark and Sweden. Christina had married the Duke of Milan at the age of thirteen and was now, at sixteen, a widow. Her Scandinavian connections mattered less than her title as Duchess of Milan – the duchy which held the key to northern Italy and which both Francis and Charles regarded as crucial in their power struggle with each other. The Duchess was in Brussels, and the English ambassador there sent home a glowing description of her beauty, charm and grace. Burning with ardour, Henry sent one of the gentlemen of his Privy Chamber, Philip Hoby, to interview her secretly, and with Hoby went Henry's favourite painter, Hans Holbein the Younger.

Holbein had first come to England in 1526 under the patronage of Sir Thomas More. His father had been a painter, but he had made a name for himself in Basle, painting his neighbour, Erasmus. It was his portrait of Erasmus that had been sent to England as an advertisement of his quality, and during his first, two-year, stay in London he painted many of the humanist circle there: More himself, of course, with his family; Sir Thomas Eliot and Sir John Gage. Through More he was given commissions by Sir Nicholas Carew, Sir Henry Guilford and Sir Brian Tuke. His fame spread. He painted the two Godsalves, Thomas and Sir John, and drew that strong-featured Cornish gentleman, Reskimer.

Christina of Milan, one of Henry's prospective wives. Holbein travelled to Brussels in 1538 to paint this lovely portrait of the sixteen-year-old widow. The match proved impossible as Henry required a papal dispensation to marry her.

Two centuries later, in a bureau in Kensington Palace, Queen Caroline – George II's consort – was to discover a great book of over eighty Holbein drawings, a portrait gallery of the courtiers of Henry VIII, their features and their personalities leaping off the page. Holbein made his living and his home among them, remaining in London until he died – of the plague – in 1543. He sketched and painted a whole generation of the English ruling class – though he did not forget his German origins. Some of his very finest London portraits were of the Hanseatic merchants, the sharp-eyed Baltic traders who lived in the turreted Steelyard on the bank of the Thames, where Cannon Street Station now stands. Though foreigners, men such as Derick Born were very much part of the life of Tudor London. The Hanse had their own alderman on the City Council, and they featured prominently in the pageantry that attended official occasions: when Anne Boleyn was crowned, for example, the Steelyard pro-

Hans Holbein and the Royal Court

In 1526, Hans Holbein the Younger arrived in England from Basle, armed with letters from Erasmus to Sir Thomas More. He began to paint portraits of More and his circle of friends. He returned briefly to Switzerland, but in 1530 he had settled firmly in England. It was from this period that he began to produce drawings of the leading members of Henry's Court, and these are still preserved at Windsor Castle. They provide us with a unique pictorial record of the period.

RIGHT Sir John Godsalve.
FAR RIGHT Holbein's self-portrait, painted in 1543, the year of his death.
BELOW LEFT Sir John Gage, one of Thomas More's closest friends.
BELOW RIGHT Reskimer, 'a Cornish gent'.

NES HOLPENIVS BA- SILEENSIS
VS EFFIGIATOR Æ: XLV.

vided butts of their fine Rhine wine to flow continuously in Thames Street, and commissioned Holbein to design a huge carnival float in the shape of an allegorical mountain. The painter obviously got on well with these Teutonic businessmen – and the finest portraits of Englishmen he painted were of similarly acute hardworking men, like Thomas Cromwell. And now, in the late 1530s, Henry VIII's insistence on a pretty wife sent Holbein off to one of Europe's great commercial centres – Brussels.

The portrait he painted of Christina, the Duchess of Milan, now hangs in the National Gallery in London: a splendid woman she looks – and looked to Henry, who duly worked himself up into a fever of amorousness. Unfortunately, her uncle Charles V was well aware that the proposed match was far more to Henry's advantage than to his own: an ironic technicality was the fact that Christina's relationship, through Charles, with Catherine of Aragon, meant that Henry could only marry her with a dispensation from the Pope: and the lady herself was far from happy with the suspicion 'that her great aunt [Catherine] was poisoned, that the second was put to death, and the third lost for lack of keeping her child-bed'. She demanded guarantees for the safety of her person, so Henry looked elsewhere.

Francis suggested Louise of Guise, the beautiful sister of Marie, now Queen of Scotland. Henry showered gifts of stag, deer and great artichokes from his gardens on the French ambassador to show his gratitude for the proposal, and Hoby and Holbein were despatched post haste to bring back their respective impressions of the lady. Then yet another Guise sister was mentioned, Renée, still more beautiful than either Louise or Marie. So, in August 1538, Hoby and Holbein were off again on their travels, charged with bringing back a portrait of Renée which could be set in a double, hinged frame alongside the picture of Louise. Henry could then compare – and anticipate – the respective delights of the two sisters. Not that these ladies had the field to themselves. There were also two cousins of Francis – Marie of Vendôme and Anne of Lorraine. Holbein painted Anne, and the French promised to obtain their own picture of Marie. Then there was Francis's own sister. It was all too complicated and important a business to be left to second-hand impressions – even from so fine a hand as Holbein's. So Henry decided that the best thing to do would be to hold a beauty parade and have all the candidates sent to Calais. The French Queen could accompany them to act as a chaperone and mistress of ceremonies, and Henry would cross the Channel to make his own personal inspection of the ladies now available in such profusion.

But France demurred. Could not the English send someone to the French Court to make the selection on Henry's behalf? 'Impossible – the thing touches me too near. I wish to see them and know them some time before deciding.' It was hardly, said the French ambassador gently, the fashion in which the knights of the Round Table treated their womenfolk – a rebuke which drew the only blush ever recorded to have reddened the Henrician cheeks. And Francis was far more blunt: it was not the custom in his country, he declared, to troop damsels of good birth like horses being reviewed for sale. Just one lady would be sent to Calais and Henry could nominate the one he wished to meet, but there would be no transactions in bulk.

Francis's defence of decency and etiquette was quite reasonable – but he was a gross fellow, as capable as Henry of forsaking manners and polite feelings when he felt like it. The real reason for his unwillingness to co-operate too enthusiastically in the King of England's spouse-hunting was the agreement that he was at this time negotiating with the Emperor Charles. In January 1539, having expressed mutual shock and horror at the news of Henry's attacks on Mother Church, particularly upon the monastic retreats of her holy men, the two great enemies concluded that familiar Renaissance preliminary to a joint declaration of war, a pact of mutual consultation. Neither would enter into any agreement with England without the other's consent, and there was talk of their ambassadors being withdrawn from London. It looked as if the long-threatened Catholic crusade was finally to commence. England was convulsed with war panic. Totally isolated, the kingdom would become, said Thomas Wriothesley, one of Cromwell's henchmen and now one of the leading Privy Councillors, 'but a morsel amongst these choppers'. In one of those great seizures that has gripped the south of the country when faced with threats like the Armada, Napoleon or Hitler, the population

LEFT St Mawes Castle, Cornwall. In 1538 Charles V and Francis I agreed to a ten-year truce which left England dangerously isolated and vulnerable to invasion. To prepare for any invasion threats, Henry ordered a whole series of coastal defences to be built at keypoints on the south and east coasts. St Mawes and Pendennis were two of his most notable castles, incorporating many advanced Continental ideas of defence.

BELOW The Kent coast around Dover was also fortified against any attacks from France. This drawing shows the defences of the harbour at Dover at the end of Henry's reign.

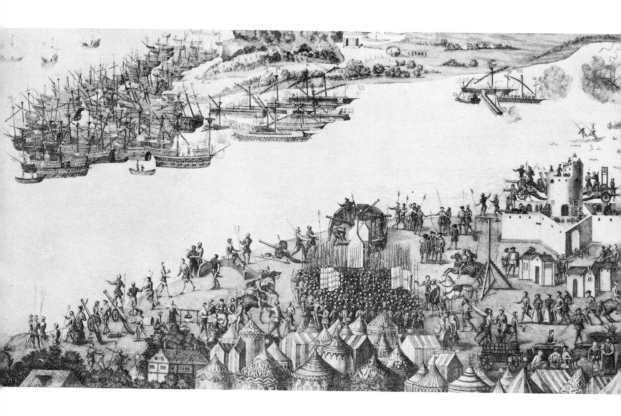

In July 1545, Henry visited Portsmouth to watch his navy meeting the French fleet in Southampton Water. Unfortunately the *Mary Rose*, the pride of Henry's navy, with its cloth-of-gold sails, turned turtle because it was top heavy. James Basire's engraving shows Henry and his army encamped in Portsmouth, and a few floating bodies to mark the site of the *Mary Rose*.

mustered, drilled, dug ditches and barricades and prepared beacons. Stone from devastated monasteries was hauled to build coastal blockhouses, merchant ships were armed, and Henry made 'very laborious and paineful journeies towards the sea coasts' to inspect royal vessels on whose strength the very salvation of the country seemed to hang.

Henry has, amongst other candidates, gone down in history as the 'Father of the English Navy' – and the title is justified. England's naval forces expanded during his reign from half a dozen ships to several score and, much more significant, many were equipped with the rows of heavy guns that, in those years, revolutionised warfare at sea. Monsters like the *Great Harry* had, instead of individual light weapons at bow and stern, tiers of gunports set into their waists, introducing for the first time to sea-battles the broadside and all that meant in terms of tactics. Henry's own personal involvement in all this is difficult to assess, but he was certainly proud of his ships: he liked to see their heavy guns 'fired again and again, marking their range, as he is very curious about matters of this kind'.

184

It looked as though, in the spring of 1539, the power and range of those guns would be far more than a matter of mere technical curiosity. Henry and Cromwell were very worried men. All the comic opera antics of the King's multiple wooings had masked a deep-rooted fear of being isolated, which had exhibited itself in several outbursts that were deadly for those they struck. One element in Henry's anxieties at his failure to produce a male heir had always been the knowledge that, in genealogical terms, his own family did not possess the strongest claim to the throne of England. Amongst the aristocracy there were families – the Staffords, the Courtenays, the Nevilles and the Poles – who were related to the Plantagenets, the dynasty of the White Rose that had ruled England for the latter part of the Middle Ages. They were not numerous and had few powerful friends, but their very existence and the comparative purity of their royal descent had always been a niggling worry to the man whose father had plucked the crown from a thorn bush on Bosworth field. In 1513 Henry had had Edmund de la Pole beheaded. In 1521 when Edward Stafford, Duke of Buckingham, exhibited too much aristocratic disdain of Wolsey's lowly birth, Henry had been quite happy to let the Cardinal exact full revenge and get the Duke executed on a flimsy treason charge. Now, as England faced Europe alone in the late 1530s, there was more reason than ever to cut down, even to uproot the White Rose – for Pope Paul III had nominated to co-ordinate the great crusade against Henry a member of one of the leading White Rose dynasties, Reginald Pole, the grandson of George, Duke of Clarence.

Reginald had once been among Henry's greatest favourites. The King had paid for his education, including a year spent studying in Padua, and had loaded him with Church preferments, though he was only a layman. Reginald had been one of the agents Henry sent to scour Europe for approval of the royal divorce, and on his return, though still not a priest, he was offered the archbishopric of York or the wealthy bishopric of Winchester. But, with separation from Rome imminent, Pole knew the price that Henry set on his offers and, unlike Fisher or More, he chose exile as the best means of not compromising his Catholic faith – though he did not refuse the pensions which Henry, with rare generosity, continued to pay him. It was not until 1536 that the true breach came when Pole, in response to an ever-trusting royal request for his views on the state of the English Church, unleashed *De Unitate Ecclesiae*, a bitter, blistering castigation of everything Henry had done. At the end of that year Pope Paul made Pole a Cardinal – though he was still not a priest, and did not take Holy Orders until he became, some twenty years later under Mary, England's last primate to pay allegiance to Rome. Worst of all, in 1537 Pole was despatched to Flanders to do what he could to abet the rebels in the North of England. Although he arrived too late, at the end of 1538 the Pope gave him the task of rallying the great Catholic powers against England's 'most cruel and abominable tyrant'.

Reginald Pole's activities, of course, simply ensured that the tyrant acted cruelly and abominably against Pole's own relatives. Henry had once admitted that he would dearly love to destroy the White Rose. Now he did so with a vengeance. Reginald's younger brother, Geoffrey was taken to the Tower and was induced, or forced, to turn King's evidence. He saved his own life at the expense of the rest of his family, for on the strength of his 'confessions' his eldest brother, Henry, Lord Montague was arrested and executed along with his cousin Henry Courtenay, Marquess of Exeter and their close friend, Sir Edward Neville. His mother, the aged Lady Margaret Pole, Countess of Salisbury, was arrested, to be executed in 1541. His small nephew, the son and heir of Montague, was despatched to the Tower never to be seen again. Exeter's little son and heir was also locked up and spent his boyhood and adolescence behind bars, not being released until Mary ascended the throne in 1553. Exeter's wife was imprisoned as well. Small wonder that Geoffrey Pole roamed Europe for ever afterwards demented with remorse, a pariah with the blood of his family on his conscience. The fact that Henry would have destroyed them all anyway and that, without the betrayal of the scarcely compromising connections between the English representatives of the White Rose and their overtly treacherous relation on the Continent, Cromwell would simply have devised another instrument of annihilation can only have made the voices inside Geoffrey Pole cry the louder.

There were, furthermore, English assassins out in Europe stalking his brother Reginald, the Cardinal, but in the event, their daggers and poison phials proved unnecessary. For, despite all his show of aggression against England, the Emperor Charles was having second thoughts. He did not trust his French ally, and he had troubles enough of his own without seeking more. He informed Cardinal Pole that he considered the Turks and the Lutherans to be more urgent objects of his godly wrath than Henry VIII. And Francis's bellicosity also faded once he sat down seriously to consider the expense and risk of mounting an effective invasion across the Channel. So the spring of martial ardour mellowed into a summer of apathy, and, miraculously, by July 1539 England was obviously safe enough from any immediate threat for the crash programme of coastal defences to be called off.

Cardinal Reginald Pole, a member of the White Rose dynasty, who did so much to ensure the destruction of his own family by his bitter attacks against 'the most abominable tyrant', Henry VIII.

8 Nemesis

IN ADDITION TO the peace of mind achieved by the extinction of the last legitimate claimants to the throne, the great panic of 1539 left another, less convenient legacy to England and her King. With Charles and Francis apparently mustering vast armies across the Channel, any question of a matrimonial alliance that depended on either of them had obviously gone by the board, and the need for a third friend, however lowly, seemed paramount. So, in January 1539, an earlier mooted suggestion had been revived to marry Henry to one of the ladies of the ruling House of Cleves. This duchy, which straddled the lower Rhine, could be a thorn in the side of the Emperor Charles, if not a fatal stab in the back. And the Duke of Cleves, furthermore, was allied to the Schmalkaldic league in which the Lutheran princes of Germany had banded together against Charles, though he was not himself, much to the satisfaction of the ever-orthodox Henry, personally of the Lutheran faith.

By the middle of March 1539 Cromwell was telling his King that Princess Anne of Cleves was an incomparable beauty 'as well for the face as for the whole body'. She excelled Henry's previous passion, Christina, the Duchess of Milan, 'as the golden sun excelleth the silver moon'. His interest kindled, Henry asked Cleves for a portrait, to be told that one had been painted but six months previously – at the same time as that of Anne's equally lovely sister, Amelia. Now the prospect of a choice, of course, simply inflamed Henry's interest the more, and thenceforward the object of his quest became twofold – though he did not forsake all prudence in his enthusiasm. The English ambassadors were instructed to inspect both sisters thoroughly to make sure that the artistic impressions that the King would see were indeed authentic delineations of the ladies being offered. The ambassadors were worried that they had only glimpsed Anne and Amelia in 'monstrous habit and apparel' which afforded 'no sight neither of their faces nor their persons'. 'Why?' responded the Chancellor of Cleves. 'Would you see them naked?'

Holbein was obviously the solution and in July he set off to Cleves. By the end of August he was back with portraits of both Anne and Amelia – and it was on Anne that the royal fancy lighted. But, as is well-known, reality did not match what the

PREVIOUS PAGES The death-bed of Henry VIII, an anti-papal allegory painted in about 1548. Henry is seen gesturing to his successor, Edward. To Edward's left are members of the Council of Regency: Edward Seymour, John Dudley, Cranmer and William Russell. The Pope is shown being crushed by the Prayer Book, and in the background soldiers are destroying religious statues. The painting may well commemorate Cranmer's order for the destruction of religious images.

portrait promised – for Henry, at least. When Anne arrived in England, at the end of 1539, the King dashed down to Rochester laden with New Year's presents and an improbable disguise 'to nourish love', as he explained to Cromwell. He wanted a secret glimpse of his bride-to-be, but no sooner had he gained this than he decided that someone else could present his gifts for him. 'I am ashamed', he complained, 'that men have so praised her as they have done – and I like her not.' He told Cromwell that she was 'nothing so well as she was spoken of', and that 'if he had known before as much as he knew then, she should not have come within his realm'.

The marriage was postponed for two days as Henry debated how to rid himself of this 'Flanders mare'. In a stronger position he might have risked making 'a ruffle in the world' and refused to 'put my neck in the yoke'. But, as Cromwell pointed out, even though the immediate threat of invasion had passed, England was as isolated as ever. She simply could not afford to offend her German allies, no matter how slender their power or their friendship. 'My Lord', Henry said valiantly to his minister on his mournful marriage morning, 'if it were not to satisfy the world and my realm, I would not do that I must do this day for none earthly thing.' Such was the royal reluctance that, though he got into bed with Anne that night, Henry made not the slightest attempt to cajole her to her wifely duty. He was 'struck to the heart' by her ugliness, he reported next day, and had 'left her as good a maid as he found her'.

Within six months divorce proceedings had begun, and within seven they were completed, Anne proving remarkably compliant throughout the whole sorry proceedings. Possibly through prudence, probably through uncomplicated good nature, she meekly agreed to confirm that her marriage had not been consummated, to hand over to the English any letters that might provide her relatives with an excuse to cause trouble and to address Henry as 'brother'. Her real brother wanted her to return to Cleves, but somehow six months of loveless marriage to an irritable and tyrannical old invalid had given Anne a taste for England. She retired to the country properties Henry had given her and lived quietly and happily on amicable terms with him and his successors until 1557, when she died and was buried in Westminster Abbey – as befitted a Queen of England.

'I am ashamed that men have so praised her ... and I like her not'

It was Thomas Cromwell who suffered most from the otherwise comical affair of Henry's short-lived fourth marriage. Just a month before Anne of Cleves was told she was no longer the King of England's wife, at 3 p.m. on Saturday 10 June 1540, the captain of the guard arrested Thomas Cromwell as he sat at the Council table doing royal business among the men who knew what his fate must be. The great minister could not believe what was happening to him as Norfolk, the Duke who had pulled down Wolsey, now delightedly stripped from Cromwell the decorations that so few lowly-born men had worn before. Not scared but simply astounded and incredulously angry at what was happening to him, Cromwell threw down his hat in furious annoyance.

The picturesque explanation of his downfall has traditionally been Holbein's artistic license. The painter, it is suggested, was a German who responded to Anne of Cleves's Teutonic qualities with a sympathy no native-born Englishman would feel, and he was, perhaps, anxious to end the series of tedious matrimonial commissions of which Anne and her sister Amelia were the fourth and fifth. So to get Henry VIII rapidly married off, he produced an over-flattering portrait for whose falsehood Cromwell, the great advocate of the Cleves marriage, paid the price.

The original picture does not, unfortunately, survive to test the truth of this well-told story. But Holbein's painting of Anne which hangs in the Louvre was based on his portrait executed in Cleves, and Wotton, one of the English envoys, described the original as 'a very lively [i.e. life-like] image'. Wotton can, moreover, be taken as a reliable witness, for he seems to have been alone in criticising Anne's attractions from the beginning. In May 1539 he reported that she was not highly educated, could not sing or play any instrument, exhibited little humour or cheerfulness and spent most of her time sewing. So the pale, pretty, but definitely withdrawn and timid-looking girl in Holbein's portrait can probably be taken as a fair representation of the real person. But it would hardly accord with Holbein's acknowledged expertise to think otherwise – and certainly it was never the accuracy of the famous painting of which Henry himself complained. He objected principally to the verbal and written descriptions of the girl that he had been given – and it seems likely that Cromwell had edited these rather too optimistically. We know that he passed on several glowing reports about Anne, but there is no evidence that more querulous opinions – like Wotton's, for example – reached the King's ears until it was too late. Moreover, when Henry had set eyes on his Flanders mare, it was certainly Thomas Cromwell who vetoed his desperate schemes for a last minute retreat.

Cromwell was indeed in a weak position. Not only was he blamed for the Cleves marriage, particularly by nobles such as Norfolk – in whom he stimulated the same resentment as Wolsey – but he was also on dangerous theological ground.

For he belonged to a small group of ecclesiastical innovators, including Archbishop Cranmer, who was promoting an element of radicalism in *doctrine* quite alien to the conservative views of the King. The first attempts by the English Church to define its beliefs had resulted, in July 1536, in the *Ten Articles*, a cautious compromise between old and new. But Cromwell has added a radical twist by making sure that English-language Bibles would be placed in every parish church. Then in 1537, after the Pilgrimage of Grace, voices urging less unsettling creeds gained the upper hand and a detailed primer of faith and instruction, generally known as the *Bishops' Book*, set out orthodox opinions.

The see-sawing between the radical and conservative tendencies continued. In his Injunction of 1538 Cromwell intensified his war on 'popish and superstitious' practices, encouraging attacks on some of England's most beautiful shrines and church ornaments so that the miraculous jewelled tomb of Becket at Canterbury, one of the wonders of the medieval world, the goal of Chaucer's famous pilgrims and of many thousands more, was looted – a brief financial gain for the government, an eternal loss for the country. Then in 1539, with England about to be invaded by the legions of Rome co-ordinated by the treacherous Cardinal Pole, official doctrine played safer than ever before, and the Six Articles set out beliefs with which the Pope himself could hardly have quarrelled: the Communion bread and wine turned into the very body and blood of Christ; confessions and confessionals were upheld against Lutheran criticisms; and priests were strictly forbidden to marry – though the world knew that Archbishop

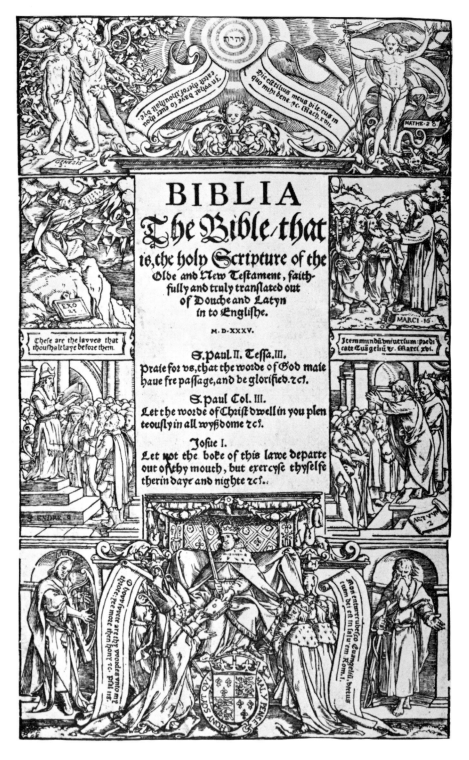

BIBLIA
The Bible, that
is, the holy Scripture of the
Olde and New Testament, faith-
fully and truly translated out
of Douche and Latyn
in to Englishe.

M·D·XXXV.

S. Paul. II. Tessa. III.
Praie for vs, that the worde of God maie
haue fre passage, and be glorified. zci.

S. Paul Col. III.
Let the worde of Christ dwell in you plen
teously in all wyssdome zcs.

Josue I.
Let not the boke of this lawe departe
out of thy mouth, but exercyse thyselfe
therin daye and nighte zc..

194

Cranmer kept as house-keeper a lady he had secretly wed in Europe and brought back to England in a trunk.

Deciding where Henry himself stood in all these bewildering shifts of theological assertion and nuance is as difficult as tracing the flow of the changes themselves, though certain facts are quite clear. His most lively concern was with dogma touching his own position and authority. When he discovered that the *King's Book*, the last religious primer to appear in his reign (in 1543), described him plainly as 'Supreme Head ... of this Church of England', he altered the text to read 'by God's law Supreme Head ... of this whole Church and congregation of England'. He crossed out the assertion in the *Bishops' Book* that he had a duty, as prince, 'to provide and care' for his people 'that all things necessary may be plenteous'. And where the book attempted to claim that he had the power to kill and execute his subjects only 'by and according to the just order of [the] laws', he altered the text to make it clear that it was simply his ministers who were under this limitation. The King himself stood above the law. Like many another Renaissance prince who embraced the Reformation, Henry saw religious innovation principally as a method of increasing his own power. It by no means implied greater liberty for his subjects – the very opposite, in fact, and Henry was deeply suspicious of any attempts to alter the hierarchy below him. Where the *Bishops' Book* had stated that all men, rich and poor, 'the free and the bond' are equal in God's eyes, the King very carefully added the crucial social proviso 'touching the soul only'.

Cromwell's enemies were shrewd enough to pick on this royal conservatism to strike down the man they hated. Norfolk, Gardiner and their supporters insinuated that the well-known religious radicalism of the minister had a sinister side: that his enthusiasm for Lutheran doctrines sprang from a fanaticism which would uphold heresy and heretics against the established social and political order. Cromwell's Lutheran friends, notably the rash and voluble Robert Barnes, were cited as examples of this. Cromwell was alleged, moreover, to have asserted fervently that Barnes preached the truth, and that even if the King turned from it 'yet I would not turn, and if the king did turn, and all his people, I would fight in this field in mine own person, with my sword in my hand against him and all other'.

In a rational, balanced mood Henry would have seen these accusations for the concocted balderdash that they were. Cromwell simply was not a fanatic. Whatever his personal sympathies, and there is little evidence that they were ever as radical as Cranmer's, his creed was simply that 'he would believe even as his master the king believed'.

But Henry, in the summer of 1540, was neither rational nor balanced. He had worked himself into a frenzy of anticipation over the arrival of Anne of Cleves – a major reason for the frustration that pole-axed him when the maiden arrived. Now Norfolk was nudging towards the King a sensual, provocative young girl of nineteen, Catherine Howard, the Duke's niece. Like two of her predecessors she had caught Henry's fancy as a maid-of-honour to the Queen she was to supplant, but there the resemblance ended, for never was Henry VIII so seduced as by Catherine Howard. She was immodest and voluptuous in a style not even Anne Boleyn had indulged, had certainly enjoyed lovers before ever she came to Court, and was vigorously aided and abetted by her relatives – and by Stephen Gardiner. The Bishop of Winchester, scenting Cromwell's blood in his nostrils, turned pander and encouraged the King and Catherine to make assignations in his house on the South Bank when tongues began to wag about the lovers' frequent journeys to the Norfolk residence.

Catherine's relatives vouched 'for her pure and honest condition' and advised her carefully 'how to behave' and 'in what sort to entertain the king's highness and how often'. But had she been the Scarlet Woman herself it is doubtful whether Henry would have noticed, so smitten was he. In his blind infatuation he even showered his good-will on Cromwell, raising him in April 1540 to the peerage and making him Lord Chamberlain of the Household. But the new Earl of Essex knew how brief his enjoyment of these dignities – and his life – must be. His fatal insistence on the match with Cleves had had as one motive his very reluctance to allow Norfolk, or any other noble, to capture the King through another Anne Boleyn. Now that had happened, and the intended victim of the aristocratic backlash was well aware what to expect. Cromwell's fate was sealed. All in the same summer month, in July 1540, Anne of Cleves was divorced, Catherine and Henry were married,

Stephen Gardiner, Bishop of Winchester, from a portrait in Hardwick Hall.

196

STEEVEN GARDNER

198

Norfolk, Gardiner and their faction seized control of the Council, Thomas Cromwell was executed and the 'heretics' who were the pretext for his downfall were judicially murdered, the bewildered and baffled Robert Barnes asking just before he was consigned to the flames what on earth his crime had been. The sheriff in charge of the burning had no answer, nor had the onlookers – and nor, probably, had Henry.

OPPOSITE Holbein's designs for jewellery.

But then he did not care. He had a new woman. And, though it chimes all too neatly with the old caricature of the womanising bluff King Hal, it must be admitted that in the summer of 1540, for the moment at least, the gain of Catherine Howard mattered more to Henry VIII than the loss of one of the most able, industrious and loyal statesmen that England has ever known.

Men had been getting used, slowly, to the idea that their King might die. In 1538 his draining ulcer had suddenly clogged, and a clot of blood caused a blockage in his lungs which, for nearly a week, made Henry black in the face and speechless. But now in 1540, with his young bride, he seemed a new man. The raptures of love with a girl thirty years his junior transported him. His headaches, his suppurating legs, his ever more unwieldy bulk, all were forgotten in a whirlwind of early rising, hunting and feasting. 'He finds himself in much better health', said the French ambassador, who confessed he had 'never seen the King in such good spirits or in so good a humour.'

His teenage Queen was showered with jewels – in the Christmas and New Year celebrations of 1540 alone with a 'square containing 27 table diamonds and 26 clusters of pearls', a brooch constructed of 33 diamonds and 60 rubies with an edge of pearl and, to warm her pretty little hands in draughty Tudor corridors and chambers, a 'muffler of black velvet furred with sables containing 38 rubies and 572 pearls'. Henry bestowed upon her, among other lands, the castles, lordships and manors which had once belonged to Jane Seymour – together with the estates of the late Thomas Cromwell. The Court of Henry VIII enjoyed an Indian summer of parties, joustings and feasts as prolonged and sumptuous as any it had known before, and its new young Queen, so recently the disregarded country daughter of a Howard n'er-do-well, revelled in her sudden opulence and good fortune. She even befriended Henry's shy

199

and ungainly 'beloved sister', Anne of Cleves, dancing with her and joining with her as host to the King at a special dinner *à trois*, a bizarre little gathering which, apparently, gave much pleasure to the participants.

But Catherine was not always so politic. Pampered, thoughtless and licentious, she was embarking on the incontinent path that led her to the block after less than eighteen months of marriage. Her adolescence had been precocious in a society where girls, usually under the strict eye of their parents, had little chance of sexual experience until they were safely married off. Her mother died before she was ten and her father, Lord Edmund Howard, a younger brother of Norfolk's, was a shiftless fellow who abandoned her to the care of her step-grandmother, the Dowager Duchess of Norfolk. This vinegary old matriarch seems to have left Catherine very much to her own devices, and before long the girl was making love with her music teacher behind the altar of the Duchess's chapel and responding with equal generosity to the advances of her handsome and dashing cousin, Francis Dereham. When she became Henry's Queen she invited Dereham to Court to become, of all things, her private secretary. And she also flirted openly with young courtiers like Thomas Paston and Thomas Culpepper junior, two gentlemen of the Privy Chamber. In all these *affaires*, Catherine was aided and abetted by the matron of her suite, Lady Rochford, a meddling woman who seems to have taken almost pathological pleasure in smuggling lovers into her lady's bedchamber, and who had evidently learnt nothing from the fate of her own husband, George Boleyn, executed for alleged incest with his sister Anne. If a Queen could be condemned for so unsubstantiated an indiscretion, how much the more peril was incurred by nightly adulteries involving comings-and-goings through the royal apartments that were inevitably witnessed by a growing number of servants.

When, in the summer of 1541, Henry embarked on a royal progress to the North – his only royal visit to those parts – Culpepper came too. At every stopping place – Greenwich, Hatfield, Lincoln, Pontefract and York – he, Lady Rochford and Catherine reconnoitred the architecture and location of the back stairs and hidden entrances to the Queen's bedroom. The trio took positive pleasure in the catastrophic risks they were running, revelling in the occasions when Culpepper had had to pick the lock of the Queen's suite or lurk on the backstairs listening for the sound of the guards passing by. As Henry received the homage of his Northern subjects, he was being cuckolded by one of his courtiers with energetic regularity.

That is probably the key to the whole tragedy, for, before her marriage, Catherine had developed appetites which her husband simply could not satisfy. There has never been any evidence that Henry was an especially gifted lover. He certainly could not stand comparison with, say, Charles II. Indeed, the ease with which Anne Boleyn held off his advances, and his preference for wives rather than mistresses, would seem to indicate that his obsession with the procreation of legitimate successors haunted not only his political and religious activities but his sex life as well. He regarded the marriage bed as existing for the begetting of children rather than for voluptuous gymnastics – and, of course, by the time Henry married Catherine Howard, he was hardly the shape for prodigious feats of amorous exertion in any case, whatever his ambitions may or may not have been in that direction. Always a moody, selfish man, Henry was becoming more and more irascible as old age and almost total immobility overtook him – by no means the romantic and persistent style of lover that Catherine's hectic adolescence had taught her to consider the norm. To be chained for life to an obese invalid with legs that oozed pus cannot have been an attractive proposition for the plump, vivacious girl, and she found it hard to pretend that she enjoyed it. She had to act as nursemaid, when, in March 1541, after and perhaps as a result of Henry's efforts at early rising and high living, the royal ulcer closed up as it had done in 1538. The King fell into an agonised black gloom that lasted for weeks.

But when Henry was, finally, told of the indiscretions of his rash young consort, his reaction was surprising. He refused to believe a single word, and, more in amusement than anger, ordered the punishment of the fellow who presumed to concoct such a far-fetched tale. This man, John Lassells, had heard through his sister of Catherine's rompings in the household of the Dowager Duchess and, while Henry was in the North, had laid his information before the three Councillors left in London: Archbishop Cranmer, Thomas Audley the Lord Chancellor, and Edward Seymour, the Earl of Hertford. All were hostile to Norfolk and obviously delighted at the tenor of the news, but neither Audley, who had risen from being the first Speaker of the Reformation Parliament, nor Hertford, very much the coming man, who owed his comparatively recent eminence to his sister Jane and the fact that he was thus uncle to Henry's sole legitimate heir, felt inclined to face their master with the news. It was Cranmer who had to undertake the unpleasant task, and even he could not bring himself 'to express the same to the King's Majesty by word of mouth'.

Henry's almost lighthearted spurning of the explosive epistle that his Archbishop handed him was not of a piece with his habitual death-dealing wrath, but it was true to his character just the same. The essence of the whole sad business was that Henry was a failing man who could no longer satisfy a young bride. Not until several weeks of quiet investigation had confirmed the truth of the allegations did Henry's humiliation manifest itself as furious indignation – and that rapidly gave way to blubbering self-pity: the King wept openly before his Council, his blustering deflated, a sagging, crippled, grey old man.

Manox, Catherine's music teacher, confessed he 'had commonly used to feel the secrets and other parts of the Queen's body', Dereham that 'he had known her carnally many times, both in his doublet and hose between the sheets and in naked bed'. Catherine herself admitted that before she met Henry, Dereham had often 'lain with me, sometimes in his doublet and, as I do think, his hose, but I mean naked when his hose were put down'. Confusing precision – but at this stage the Council knew nothing of Catherine's adventures since she married Henry, and it seemed possible for a time that excessively spectacular scandal might be avoided by a quick divorce on the grounds of a pre-existing agreement to marry between Dereham and Catherine. Dereham certainly pleaded innocence on the grounds of such an engagement, but Catherine absolutely denied any promise of marriage and sensing their prey's weakness, the Council, including Norfolk and Gardiner, who had abandoned their young protégée at the first sign of trouble, were soon on the trail of Culpepper and Lady Rochford. Hoping to save her neck, the lady gave her opinion 'that

Culpepper hath known the Queen carnally, considering all things that she [Lady Rochford] hath heard and seen between them' – and thus condemned herself for complicity.

Christmas 1541 was a gloomy feast. Dereham and Culpepper were executed before it, their heads being impaled on London Bridge: the deaths of Catherine and Lady Rochford followed in the New Year, their condemnation being set out in an Act of Attainder which also made it a treasonable offence for any woman whose previous life had been unchaste to marry the King. 'Few, if any, ladies now at court would henceforth aspire to such an honour', commented Chapuys. But, in less cynical mood, he summed up well the dull melancholia in which the whole episode enveloped Henry. The King's 'case', he said 'resembles very much that of the woman who cried more bitterly at the loss of her tenth husband than she had on the death of the other nine put together ... the reason being that she had never buried one of them without being sure of the next, but that after the tenth husband she had no other one in view, hence her sorrow and her lamentations'. Henry was not mourning Catherine – he was grieving for himself.

War was his last, hopeless, attempt to recapture his youth. In the summer of 1542, only two score months after they were swearing eternal friendship to each other and death to England, the Emperor Charles and King Francis were again at each other's throats. It seemed the ideal opportunity for Henry to achieve his eternal and unoriginal ambition to reconquer England's empire in France. But first he had to eliminate any danger from Scotland. He did not want to risk a war on two fronts. Throughout the summer of 1542 English troops were built up along the Scottish border and the young King, James V, was presented with a treaty to sign that would have made his country effectively England's satellite. When Scotland refused to have anything to do with such proposals, Norfolk, more than eager to erase the stain of saddling Henry with two adulterous nieces, led the English army on a six-day raid towards Kelso, burning, looting and leaving savage devastation in his wake. The following month James retaliated. The Scottish army, far superior to the forces at Henry's disposal, marched south, but got bogged down in the marshes of Solway Moss and was

'Culpepper hath known the Queen carnally'

203

routed. Few soldiers on either side were killed, but hundreds of Scottish prisoners were captured, including many nobles. When James heard of the defeat he was heart-broken: the disgrace of it killed him, and his throne was left to his week-old daughter, whose life was to end in tragedy as it began – Mary, Queen of Scots.

Had Henry marched North he could have conquered. But sixteenth-century monarchs did not wage war like twentieth-century nations. There was no honour to be gained from sending troops into a helpless country whose sovereign was a baby girl – and Henry's principal objective was northern France. So devious manœuvrings were entered into, which reached fruition on 1 July 1543. On that date at Greenwich Scotland's ambassadors agreed to a treaty of marriage between their infant Queen Mary and Henry's heir Edward. And, in the meantime, five thousand English troops crossed the Channel in preparation for the main exercise, the assault on France. Charles and Henry agreed that they would each, by 20 June of the following year, put an army of forty-two thousand in the field. The Emperor would lead his troops through Champagne while Henry would march down the Somme to Paris. 1544 would be for the English King the *annus mirabilis* that would see him crowned on the throne of his long-lost second kingdom.

But Scotland determined otherwise. 'Under the sun live not more beastly and unreasonable people than be here of all degrees', complained Sir Ralph Sadler, one of Cromwell's young men, who had been given the job of making the Scots fulfill the terms of the treaty signed at Greenwich. By Christmas 1543 the Scottish Parliament in nationalistic resentment at the overbearing presumption of its southern neighbour had solemnly annulled all its agreements with England and renewed all its treaties of friendship with France.

Incensed with fury at what he considered to be a gross betrayal, and needing desperately to knock out Scotland before he could turn on France, Henry instructed his Northern commander-in-chief Edward Seymour (Lord Hertford) to wreak bloodthirsty vengeance on Edinburgh, Leith and St Andrews so that 'the upper stone may the nether and not one stick stand by another'. Hertford rightly suggested that such a raid would in the long run rouse the Scots rather than quell

James V of Scotland, Henry's nephew. In 1542, the Scots were disastrously defeated at Solway Moss and the disgrace broke James's heart. He died soon after, leaving his week-old daughter Mary as heir to his throne.

them, but he was overruled and, in ten spring days of violence in 1544, performed most of what he was ordered.

Henry could, for the moment at least, safely turn to the project of which, said the Privy Council, he had thought to the exclusion of all else, both night and day. He insisted that he should lead his armies into France in person, if only because Charles was intending to march at the head of his own Imperial forces. On 14 July 1544, the King was borne into Calais in a litter – the fourth visit of his life, and the second in time of war – and on 18 September, Boulogne was captured. But Henry had never attempted to march on Paris as he had promised Charles, who promptly made his own peace with Francis and indulged in a campaign of recrimination which brought Anglo-Imperial relations to near breaking-point the following year. And the English army, badly in need of a Wolsey to organise its food, drink, tents and supplies, and under the tired generalship of those elderly war-horses Norfolk and Suffolk, was close to mutiny. By the middle of October 1544 Henry was happy to sue for peace with France, not least because he was catastrophically impoverished by his own belligerence. He had expected his campaign to cost a quarter of a million pounds. It had cost nearly three times that, and hostilities were to drag on for another two years at as much cost again. In these last years of his reign Henry spent some two million pounds on war – probably ten times as much as the expenditure on the French campaigns that had followed his accession.

Monastic lands that Cromwell had retained to bolster the Crown's finances were now sold off with reckless abandon: some £800,000 came into the Court of Augmentations, which handled these sales, between 1542 and 1547, most of it passing straight on to the pockets of military suppliers. Now began the great debasement of England's coinage which must have yielded well over a third of a million pounds – at the cost of ever more rapidly spiralling prices. The man who had probably been but five years earlier the richest King in Europe, now had to go cap in hand to the Antwerp money market to raise at ten and fourteen per cent loans which totalled £75,000 at his death. And, on top of all this, Henry still had to impose upon his country taxes and forced loans heavier than any subsidies that had ever been extracted before. Wolsey's extortions were

ABOVE Lady Catherine Willoughby de Eresby, whom Charles Brandon married in 1533, after the death of Mary Tudor. Catherine, who was fourteen when she married, was the daughter of Doña Maria de Salinas, one of Catherine of Aragon's favourite ladies-in-waiting. Drawing by Holbein.

LEFT Charles Brandon, Duke of Suffolk, who was one of Henry's closest companions on the hunting field, and in the tiltyard. This portrait was painted when he was middle-aged and is in marked contrast to the portrait on page 50.

nothing compared to these levies that exceeded half a million pounds, without including the 'benevolences' screwed out of both clergy and laity with the promise, but no honest intention, of repayment.

It has often been remarked that the Dissolution of the Monasteries presented Henry VIII with a glorious opportunity to construct in England a system of education and welfare the envy of the world, and that he squandered it on war. That criticism is unfair, for it blames Henry for not being something he never was nor could have become. He never claimed to be a philanthropist, or even to care very deeply for his country and people, except insofar as they were his own possessions and thus reflections of his glory. But he did care passionately about the power and majesty of his monarchy, and on that ground he must stand condemned, for the fortune that Henry VIII dissipated on war destroyed the financial independence of the Crown and permanently diminished the authority of England's Kings and Queens. Posterity has been thankful for that, but more than a few of Henry's royal successors have not.

The reign that had burst upon England with the radiance of the rising sun was ending in shadows. Dark intrigues at a Court where it had never been prudent to trust to appearances muddied into plots whose obscurity has baffled historians, let alone the men so fatally struck down. Norfolk and Gardiner, only temporarily set back by the foolishness of Catherine Howard, and incensed against the man who had first betrayed her to the King, renewed their long-standing campaign against Cranmer, Cromwell's great ally and the evangelical beacon from whose light England's reformers took hope.

'The greatest heretic in Kent'

But some tie that bound Henry to no other man, bound him to this quiet, earnest cleric, 'the greatest heretic in Kent', as he cheerfully described him. He told Cranmer what was plotted against him, and when the hunters pounced next day, the Archbishop produced a ring that Henry had given him. Confused, but unsuspecting, the accusers went to the King for adjudication, only to be castigated savagely. They had destroyed Cromwell, but they would not cut down any other faithful servants in their jealousy. Henry derived a failing old man's delight in so stirring energies more potent than his own, only to frustrate and mock them.

208

In July 1543 he had taken to wife his sixth and final Queen, Catherine Parr, a lady who had a fair record of marriages of her own. It was appropriate that the final partner of England's most-married king should be the country's most-married queen. Thirty-one years old and the daughter of a North-amptonshire knight, she had twice been widowed and was, in fact, to outlive Henry and take a fourth husband. A solid, agreeable woman who, like Jane Seymour, succeeded in reuniting the offspring of Henry's various unions into some semblance of a family, she was a good companion to sooth the declining years of a tyrant ever more self-absorbed in his illness and embittered by a loneliness he had worked a lifetime to create. Catherine was a learned, purposeful lady, recruiting noted humanists as tutors for the royal children and enjoying the company of progressive theological thinkers like Hugh Latimer and Miles Coverdale, the translator of the Bible into English. She held, indeed, daily Scripture classes of an evangelical nature for her ladies-in-waiting, and was not reluctant to expound her religious beliefs to her husband – altogether a contrast to her scarcely pious predecessor – perhaps too much of a contrast. Stephen Gardiner certainly thought so and made against Queen Catherine the same accusation he had, unsuccessfully, made against Cranmer. For Henry to tolerate Catherine's radical beliefs was 'to cherish a serpent within his own bosom', said the Bishop of Winchester. And as the King had listened to the case against Cranmer, so he heard the charges against his wife, agreed to her arrest, and even signed a bill of articles setting out her heresies. But Henry was playing a cat and mouse game again. Catherine was warned of the apparent danger she was in and duly threw herself on her husband's mercy, disowning any suggestion that she intended to force her ideas on her spouse but insisting, on the contrary, that she desired only to be instructed by him. 'And is it even so, sweetheart?' beamed Henry, all forgiveness. 'Then perfect friends we are now again as at any time heretofore.'

So, when Thomas Wriothesley came next day at Gardiner's behest to arrest Catherine as she walked in the garden of Whitehall with her husband, the Councillor was set upon by his royal master. 'Knave! arrant knave! beast! and fool!' cried Henry, delighted to be able to exercise his power, if only through caprice and deceit. As men looked more and more to the future, the King whose glory lay in the past fought desperately, and viciously, to keep some grasp on the present.

Now almost immobile, carried about by chair or litter and winched up and downstairs by machinery, cursing the ever sharpening pain of his ulcer and wracked more and more frequently by fevers, King Henry VIII was manifestly in decline. The predators who had hunted with him for so many years were sharpening their claws for the struggle all knew must come, to gain control of the sickly child due to inherit the kingdom. There was Hertford, Henry's brother-in-law and young Edward's uncle, who had reinforced his claims of kinship with solid achievements on the battlefield. Another new man was John Dudley, Viscount Lisle, son of the Dudley whom Henry had sacrificed to popular opinion at the outset of his reign. John Dudley had distinguished himself by his handling of the navy during the months between the capture of Boulogne and the treaty of peace with the French finally signed at Ardres in June 1546. By the end of that year, only a month before Henry's death, Dudley had pushed, with Hertford, to the forefront of the Council, though more by default than through any positive expression of favour by the ailing King. The Duke of Suffolk had died the previous year; Gardiner had suffered from his over-zealous onslaughts on Cranmer and Catherine, and was injudiciously obstinate in an otherwise trivial dispute with Henry over the exchange of some lands; and Norfolk, the tired old warrior with the parchment face and cold eyes, who had survived so much through so many years was, in the last few weeks of Henry's reign, suddenly cut down with the bewildering savagery he had seen destroy so many others.

The primary object of Henry's displeasure was Norfolk's eldest son Henry, Earl of Surrey, an extravagant, roistering soldier-poet who had been made a scapegoat for a few of the many deficiencies in the English campaigns around Boulogne. He was a brilliant, indiscreet young man who loved to flout conventions both trivial and important, ostentatiously refusing to eat meat in Lent, complaining openly about the power given to low-born men like Wolsey and Cromwell and, worse, boasting of his own descent from the Plantagenets. To emphasise his connections with the blood royal he had his own arms

quartered with those of Edward the Confessor.

In more settled times his arrogance might have been ignored. But for Hertford and Dudley, consolidating their power against the day of young Edward's accession, it was the lever they needed to topple Norfolk. The echoes of the White Rose were fatal. On 12 December 1546 both Surrey and his father were arrested and despatched to the Tower. Five weeks later Surrey was beheaded, and on 27 January 1547 the royal assent was given to the execution of Norfolk. He was to die next morning – a Friday.

But the old campaigner survived – just, for the Angel of Death which hovered over London that night swooped down not to the Tower but to St James's Palace where Henry VIII lay breathing feebly. His physicians did not dare tell him that the fever which gripped him was a fatal one, for to prophesy the decease of the monarch was treason by act of Parliament. But Henry had known by Christmas that his end was close. He had drawn up his Will, entrusting his kingdom and his son Edward to a Council of Regency which would, inevitably, be dominated by Hertford and Dudley. When Sir Anthony Denny, the chief gentleman of the Chamber, advised him on that cold Thursday evening 'to prepare himself to death', Henry 'disposed himself more quietly ... to consider his life past'.

Should a priest be sent for? asked Denny. Henry replied that, if he wanted anyone it would be Cranmer but that 'I will first take a little sleep and then, as I feel myself, I will advise upon the matter'. He dozed for an hour or two, then asked for the Archbishop, who arrived about midnight. The King was speechless and nearly unconscious, but he stretched out his hand to this cleric who, after the destruction of the Howards, was the only companion left from the high old days of the early 1530s when England had so proudly blazed a trail for herself in defiance of the world. Cranmer asked his master for some token, some sign that he put his trust in Christ, whereupon Henry 'holding him with his hand, did wring his hand in his as hard as he could'. And so passed away, at about two in the morning on Friday, 28 January 1547, King Henry VIII of England. He was exactly fifty-five years and seven months old and his reign had lasted for thirty-seven years and eight months.

For three days his successors kept the news of his death to

ABOVE Stained-glass panel from Barham Hall, showing the arms of the Duke of Norfolk, including the leopards of England. The Howard connections with the blood royal were to prove their downfall.

OPPOSITE Henry Howard, Earl of Surrey, as painted by Guillem Stretes in 1546. A year later he was executed for high treason involving heraldic offences – the royal arms of England can be seen on the shield in the right-hand part of the portrait.

ANNO·DNI·1546·ÆTATIS·18·SVE·29

ABOVE Henry VIII in old age, showing how heavy and gross his features had become.

RIGHT Henry VIII's will, which was affirmed with his stamp on 30 December 1546. The document provided a Council of Regency for Edward and settled the succession to the Crown, after Edward and his heirs, to first Mary and then Elizabeth.

214

In the name of god and of the glorious and blessed
virgin our Lady Saint mary and of all the holy
company of heaven We Henry by the grace
of god king of England france and Ireland
defender of the faith and in erth ymedyately
under god the Supreme hed of the Churche of
England and Ireland of that name the viijth
callyng to our remembraunce the great gifte and
benefitt of Almightie god geven unto us in this
transitory lief geven unto him our moost lowly
and humble thanke knowledging our selff insufficient
in any part to deserve or recompence the same
But fere that we have not worthely receyved
the same And considering further also to our selff
that we be as all mankind is mortall and born
in sinne Beleving neverthelesse and hoping that every
creature livyng here in this transitory and
wretched woorld under god dying in stedfast
and perfait faith endevoring and exercising himself
to execute in his lief tyme if he have leasure suche
good dedes and charitable workes as scripture comandeth
and as may be to the honour and pleasir of god

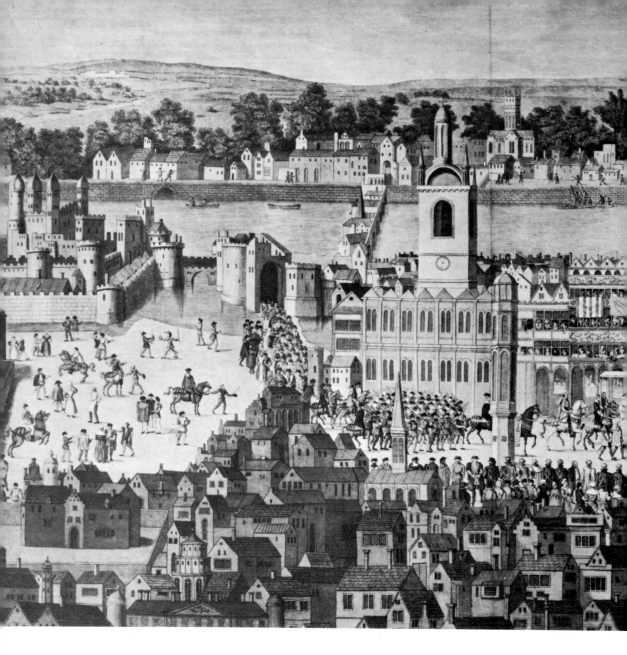

themselves, furiously debating the fate of the dangerous Duke of Norfolk who, in the end, was spared, though kept safely behind bars. Then, on Monday, 31 January 1547, Lord Chancellor Paget, in a voice choked with emotion, told the Houses of Parliament that their King was dead. On 8 February in every parish church in England was sung a solemn dirge as the mourning bells rang, and the following morning the kingdom offered up a Requiem Mass for the dead King's soul. His body was buried a week later beside Jane Seymour's according to the

The coronation procession of Edward VI in 1547, a watercolour by Grimm from a wall painting in Cowdray House, which was destroyed by fire. The illustration shows the procession leaving the

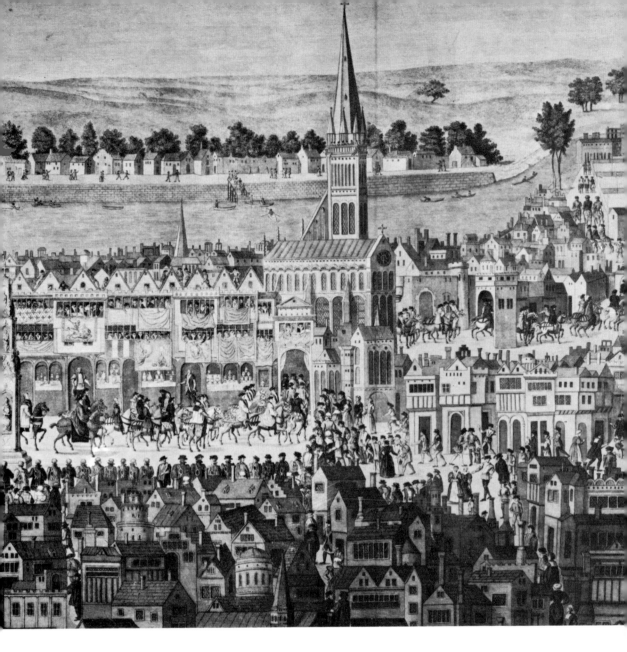

Tower and moving along East Cheap, past Bow Church into Cheapside (the spire belongs to St Paul's Cathedral), and down the Strand to Charing Cross and Westminster.

wishes set out in his Will. 'He desires that he be laid in the choir of his college at Windsor and that an altar shall be founded for the saying of daily Mass while the world shall endure.'

Though the world has endured, that altar with its daily Masses to be sung through all eternity for the departed royal soul has fared less successfully. But King Henry VIII has no need of priests and prayer to keep his memory alive.

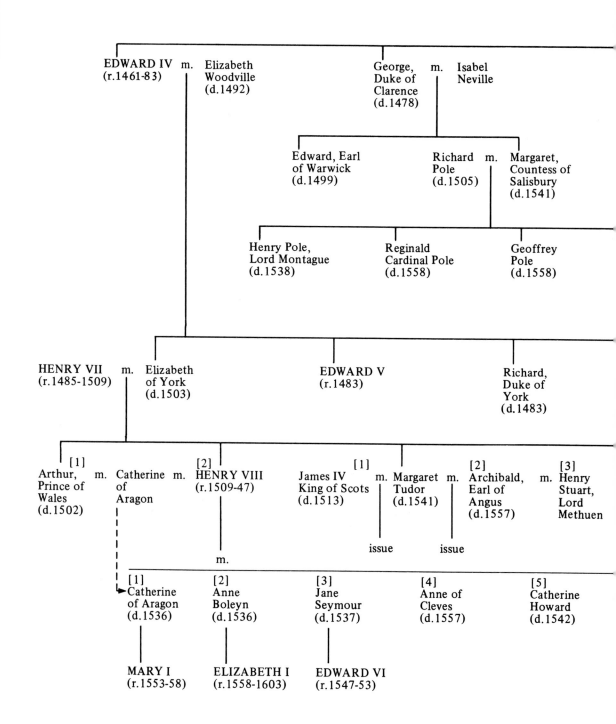

EDWARD IV m. Elizabeth
(r.1461-83)   Woodville
              (d.1492)

George, m. Isabel
Duke of   Neville
Clarence
(d.1478)

Edward, Earl
of Warwick
(d.1499)

Richard m. Margaret,
Pole   Countess of
(d.1505)   Salisbury
            (d.1541)

Henry Pole,
Lord Montague
(d.1538)

Reginald
Cardinal Pole
(d.1558)

Geoffrey
Pole
(d.1558)

HENRY VII m. Elizabeth
(r.1485-1509) of York
               (d.1503)

EDWARD V
(r.1483)

Richard,
Duke of
York
(d.1483)

[1]
Arthur, m. Catherine m. HENRY VIII
Prince of   of   (r.1509-47)
Wales   Aragon
(d.1502)

[2]

[1]
James IV m. Margaret m. Archibald, m. Henry
King of Scots Tudor   Earl of   Stuart,
(d.1513)   (d.1541)   Angus   Lord
                          (d.1557)   Methuen

[2]

[3]

issue   issue

m.

[1]
Catherine
of Aragon
(d.1536)

[2]
Anne
Boleyn
(d.1536)

[3]
Jane
Seymour
(d.1537)

[4]
Anne of
Cleves
(d.1557)

[5]
Catherine
Howard
(d.1542)

MARY I
(r.1553-58)

ELIZABETH I
(r.1558-1603)

EDWARD VI
(r.1547-53)

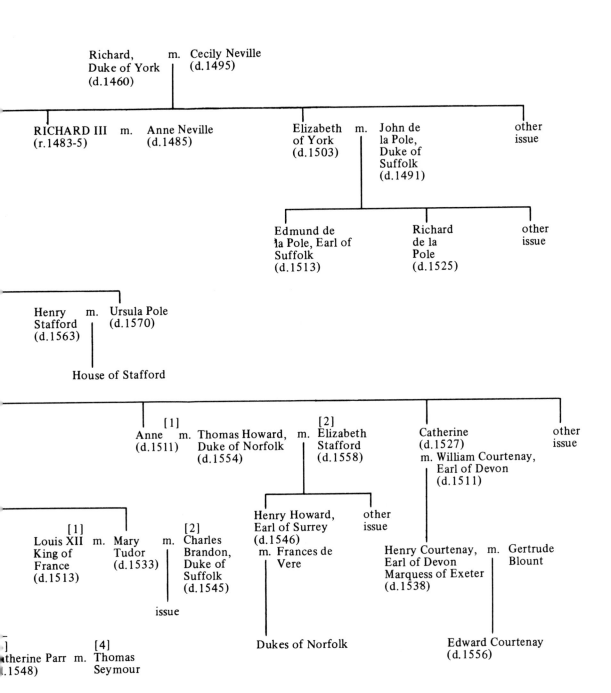

Richard,
Duke of York
(d.1460)
m. Cecily Neville
(d.1495)

RICHARD III
(r.1483-5)
m. Anne Neville
(d.1485)

Elizabeth
of York
(d.1503)
m. John de
la Pole,
Duke of
Suffolk
(d.1491)

other
issue

Edmund de
la Pole, Earl of
Suffolk
(d.1513)

Richard
de la
Pole
(d.1525)

other
issue

Henry
Stafford
(d.1563)
m. Ursula Pole
(d.1570)

House of Stafford

[1]
Anne
(d.1511)
m. Thomas Howard,
Duke of Norfolk
(d.1554)
m. [2]
Elizabeth
Stafford
(d.1558)

Catherine
(d.1527)
m. William Courtenay,
Earl of Devon
(d.1511)

other
issue

[1]
Louis XII
King of
France
(d.1513)
m. Mary
Tudor
(d.1533)
m. [2]
Charles
Brandon,
Duke of
Suffolk
(d.1545)

Henry Howard,
Earl of Surrey
(d.1546)
m. Frances de
Vere

other
issue

Henry Courtenay,
Earl of Devon
Marquess of Exeter
(d.1538)
m. Gertrude
Blount

issue

Dukes of Norfolk

Edward Courtenay
(d.1556)

[1]
atherine Parr
.1548)
m. [4]
Thomas
Seymour

Select bibliography

Bindoff, S. T., *Tudor England* (1950)

Bowle, John, *Henry VIII: A Biography* (1964)

Bruce, Marie Louise, *The Making of Henry VIII* (1977)

Cavendish, George, *The Life and Death of Cardinal Wolsey*, ed. Sylvester, Early English Text Society (1959)

Chamberlain, S., *Hans Holbein the Younger* (1913)

Chamberlin, F., *The Private Character of Henry VIII* (1932)

Devereux, E. J., 'Elizabeth Barton and Tudor Censorship', *Bull. John Rylands Library*, 49 (1966)

Dickens, A. G., *Thomas Cromwell and the English Reformation* (1959)
Heresy and the Origins of English Protestantism (1962)
The English Reformation (1964)

Dietz, F., *English Public Finance 1485–1558*, University of Illinois Studies in the Social Sciences (1920)

Doernberg, E., *Henry VIII and Luther* (1961)

Elton, G. R., *The Tudor Revolution in Government* (1953)
England Under the Tudors (2nd ed., 1974)
'The Commons' Supplication of 1532: Parliamentary manoeuvres in the reign of Henry VIII', *English Historical Review*, LXVI (1951)
'Thomas Cromwell's Decline and Fall', *Cambridge Hist. Journal*, X (1951)
'King or Minister? The man behind the Henrician reformation', *History*, XXXIX (1954)
'The political creed of Thomas Cromwell', *T.R.H.S.*, 5th ser., VI (1956)

Flügel, J. C., 'On the Character and Married Life of Henry VIII' in *Psychoanalysis and History* (1963)

Foxe, John, *Acts and Monuments* (*The Book of Martyrs*), ed. Pratt (8 vols, 1874)

Ganz, P., 'Holbein and Henry VIII', *Burlington Magazine*, LXXIII (1943)

Huizinga, J., *Erasmus of Rotterdam* (1952)

Jordan, W. K., *Philanthropy in England 1480–1660* (1959)

Kelly, M. J., 'The Submission of the Clergy', *T.R.H.S*, 5th ser., XV (1965)

Knowles, M. D., *The Religious Orders in England. III: The Tudor Age* (1959)

Knox, D. B., *The Doctrine of Faith in the Reign of Henry VIII* (1961)

Levine, M., 'The Last Will and Testament of Henry VIII: a Reappraisal Reappraised', *Historian* (1964)

Luke, M. D., *Catherine the Queen* (1967)

Mathew, D., *The Courtiers of Henry VIII* (1970)

McConica, J. K., *English Humanists and Reformation Politics under Henry VIII and Edward VI* (1965)
Erasmus (1991)

Mackie, J. D., *The Earlier Tudors 1485–1558* (1952)

McNalty, A. S., *Henry VIII, a difficult patient* (1952)

Marcus, G. J., *A Naval History of England. I: The Formative Years* (1961)

Marius, Richard, *Thomas More* (1984)

Mattingly, G., *Catherine of Aragon* (1950)
   Renaissance Diplomacy (1955)

Muller, J. A., *Stephen Gardiner and the Tudor Reaction* (1926)

Nelson, W., *John Skelton Laureate* (1939)

Oppenheim, M., *History of the Administration of the Royal Navy* (1896)

Paul, J. E., *Catherine of Aragon and Her Friends* (1966)

Plowden, Alison, *The House of Tudor* (1976)

Pollard, A. F., *Henry VIII* (1951)
   Wolsey (new ed., 1953)

Reed, A. W., *Early Tudor Drama* (1926)

Reynolds, E. E., *St John Fisher* (1955)

Ridley, Jasper, *Thomas Cranmer* (1962)
   Henry VIII (1984)

Rival, Paul, *The Six Wives of Henry VIII* (1971)

Roper, William, *The Lyfe of Sir Thomas Moore, knight*, ed. Hitchcock, Early
   English Text Society (1935)

Scarisbrick, J., *Henry VIII* (1968)

Simon, Joan, *Education and Society in Tudor England* (1966)

Smith, Lacey Baldwin, *A Tudor Tragedy. The Life and Times of Catherine
   Howard* (1961)
   Henry VIII: The Mask of Royalty (1971)
   'The Last Will and Testament of Henry VIII: a question of perspective',
   Journal of British Studies, ii (1962)
   'Henry VIII and the Protestant Triumph', *American Hist. Review*, LXXI
   (1966)

Starkey, David, *The Reign of Henry VIII: Personalities and Politics* (1985)

Stow, John, *A Survey of London*, ed. Kingsford (2 vols, 1908)

Summerson, J., *Architecture in Britain 1530–1830* (1958)

Thompson, P., *Sir Thomas Wyatt and His Background* (1964)

Tjernagel, N. S., *Henry VIII and the Lutherans* (1965)

Wernham, R. B., *Before the Armada: The Growth of English Foreign Policy
   1485–1588* (1966)

Wilding, Peter, *Thomas Cromwell*, 1935

Williamson, J. A., *The Voyages of the Cabots and the English Discovery of
   North America under Henry VII and Henry VIII* (1929)
   The Tudor Age (3rd ed., 1964)

Index